The New Manager's Starter Kit

The New Manager's Starter Kit

Essential Tools for Doing the Job Right

Robert Crittendon

AMACOM
American Management Association
New York • Atlanta • Chicago • Kansas City • San Francisco • Washington, D.C.
Brussels • Mexico City • Tokyo • Toronto

This publication is designed to provide accurate and authoritative
information in regard to the subject matter covered. It is sold with the
understanding that the publisher is not engaged in rendering legal,
accounting, or other professional service. If legal advice or other expert
assistance is required, the services of a competent professional person
should be sought.

Library of Congress Cataloging-in-Publication Data

Crittendon, Robert.
    The new manager's starter kit : essential tools for doing the job right /
    Robert Crittendon.
       p.   cm.
    Includes index.
    ISBN 0-8144-7135-8
    1. Executive ability.   2. Management.   I. Title.

    HD38.2 .C75   2001
    658.4—dc21

                                 2001034334

Printing number

10 9 8 7 6 5 4 3 2 1

This book is respectfully dedicated to the officers at Beckman, who made management an exciting contact sport; to my former colleagues and current golf cronies, who provide perspective and good advice with uncommonly good nature; and to my supportive wife and family, who help me enjoy the journey and find a little magic every day.

CONTENTS

INTRODUCTION

In the interest of saving you time and money, let me tell you what this book is and isn't. It's a collection of personal observations for the serious manager—observations about business practices and the way people go about making decisions that influence their businesses. In essence, it's about relationships and the "people" side of many important business transactions.

That means that it isn't a textbook or procedures manual or history book. You won't find many specific names and places recorded, because that isn't the point. Reconstructing the event is not as important as understanding the principle involved. And although these truths are not always self-evident, they are universal. So universal, in fact, that you'll probably see people you know in some of these examples. Better yet, you may recognize yourself and come to a new understanding of how you meet your management challenges. If not a giant helping hand for new managers, this book is at least a secure stepping-stone to assist you in finding your own way up the slope.

The maxims and instructions contained herein are not included for their interest or novelty value. They're here for their utility value. Each lesson is a lesson learned from real-life experience (some more painful than others). These experiences were acquired during my many years at Beckman Instruments, but they contain something that should be useful for you to unpack and plug into your own office or personal environment. That's why this book is particularly practical for the new or emerging manager. I am not interested in theoretical assumptions and have only included lessons I have learned by doing and observing. As Yogi Berra said, "Sometimes you can observe a lot just by watching."

Before you begin, let me remove several myths about the book that might impede your reading.

- ■ *Myth 1. This book had to be written.* Let me assure you that I am under no such delusion. Aside from the Holy Scriptures, I know of few works that had to be written. These pages contain lessons you would probably learn yourself, given time (hopefully less than forty years) and the opportunity to interact with good companies of various sizes and the seasoned executives good companies attract. This book may tell you some things you already know. Not to worry. Review is always beneficial, and—like a commercial pilot going through a preflight checklist—you may find something you'd missed heretofore. It might even turn out to be something that will keep the wings from falling off your business later on.

- ■ *Myth 2. This book wrote itself.* No way. Admittedly, it was easier to write because I didn't have to make up anything. Since it is recorded experience and observation, it was all inside my skull. But digging these recollections out of the caverns of the mind is not as easy as it sounds, and the experiences took more time to dislodge than I had anticipated. To those who have pestered me to write a book, I hope the wait was worth it.

- ■ *Myth 3. One size fits all.* Caution: This book may not apply to all businesses or all organizations of all sizes. It stands a better chance than most, however, because it is focused on what you might call "*human*agement"— face-to-face human responses to the most pressing everyday management situations, not specific e-commerce problems or software programs or computer-aided decisions. For that reason, some of the same basic principles may apply in any enterprise and many situations, including implementing a business plan for your church or organizing your local garden club's annual flower show.

Finally, each of the nine chapters is a lesson on a major management topic. Some have asked, "Why nine lessons; why not twenty or thirty?" The main reason is that I have tried to stick to the "vital few" and not trivialize the whole by including marginal dissertations on lesser subjects. In addition, I am trying to provide tools that you can use, and I do not wish to add so many tools that you'll be unable to lift the toolbox. Take these, use them, and come back if you need more.

1

MANAGING
YOURSELF

One must have the adventurous daring to accept oneself as a bundle of possibilities and undertake the most interesting game in the world—making the most of one's best.

—*Harry Emerson Fosdick*

The first rule is to arm yourself with a personal code of conduct. The second rule is to never break the first rule. Guidelines include having commitment (i.e., if it's worth doing, it's worth doing right), making communications an obsession, and—strangely enough—never taking yourself too seriously.

ESTABLISH RULES THAT GOVERN YOUR LIFE

Managing yourself is the hard part. It's the first task and the most difficult—but it can be made easier if you bring a little order to the assignment, like establishing a personal set of rules or a code of conduct for your business life, as well as for your personal life. True, if you haven't developed a set of business ethics by now, you're probably in deep trouble (or awaiting indictment). But you may have developed one and just not be aware of it. To remedy that, you should take the time to write your rules down. Remember that the mere act of writing them down establishes those principles in your consciousness as being important to you and is already a big step toward activating them. In her book *Write It Down, Make It Happen*, Dr. Henriette Klauser, a communications and writing productivity specialist, says that "life is a narrative that you have a hand in writing" and that writing down your goals and beliefs will prime your brain to pay attention to them.

We are not talking here about business goals and objectives or personal goals and objectives. We're talking about personal ethics and rules, the ideology you live by. Writing personal guidelines as a code to set limits on your behavior isn't a product of present-day psychologists. It's been going on through the ages and it's a practice you've probably bumped into while examining the lives of great leaders. George Washington, for instance, identified strong leadership values by studying noteworthy role models among the Virginia gentry. At the age of thirteen he wrote down 110 standards of gentlemanly behavior that he entitled "Rules of Civility and Decent Behavior in Company and Conversation." Throughout his life, Washington attempted to live up to those character components. Then, as now, character counts.

> Write down your personal code of conduct to keep
> it in your conscious mind.

Just as the father of our country studied others as role models, it's okay to borrow ideas from others for your code of conduct—but only if you accept them unconditionally. Let's assume that you already embrace basic tenets such as the Ten Commandments as the foundation for your value system. That's a fine start, but now you want to personalize additional rules that are important to you. These are standards against which you will measure many of life's important decisions facing you each day. Let's try out a few examples, just to get you rolling:

■ *Rule 1. If it's worth doing, it's worth doing right!* I
know. It sounds way too simple, but you'd be amazed
at how this rule influences the way in which you attack
an assignment and how much of yourself you put into
it. Time and again, we have seen how the lack of
commitment to "doing it right" has spelled disaster.
Examples are the sloppy project planning, the

improperly written medical prescription, the missed maintenance schedule, the careless accounting mistake, and other hasty shortcuts with calamitous effect. They also beg the question: "If you don't have time to do it right the first time, where will you find the time to do it over?"

"Doing things right" is a way of life. Vince Lombardi, legendary coach of the Green Bay Packers, said it this way: "You don't just do things right once in a while. You do them right all of the time!" Sixteen centuries earlier, Aristotle—"the teacher of those who know"—extolled the importance of making excellence a habit. It takes real gut-wrenching determination, which many managers may not want to embrace.

One of my mentors, Dr. Arnold Beckman, led a storied life and followed a strong set of personal rules. He was a blacksmith's son who grew up in a small Illinois farming community and turned his natural inquisitiveness into a career as one of the world's leading inventors of scientific instruments. That earned him a fortune and a place alongside Thomas Edison and Alexander Graham Bell in the National Inventors Hall of Fame. Among his seven lifelong personal rules was this: "Always strive for excellence. There's no substitute for it." Excellence is doing it right, unconditionally, all the time.

As with any rule, there are also caveats with this one:

1. *Make sure that what you're doing is worth doing in the first place.* No one wants to do wrong things in the right way. One of the best questions a manager should ask, and often, is: "Why are we doing this?" or, more appropriately, "Why am *I* doing this?" If you

can't answer to your satisfaction, perhaps either it isn't worth doing or someone else should be doing it.

2. *Keep the objective in front of you at all times.* During my tenure at Beckman Instruments, CEO Lou Rosso did a marvelous job of keeping corporate staff discussion on target by regularly injecting into the heat of give and take this simple comment: "Let's get back to what it is we're trying to do here." As my grandfather used to say, "You can't catch one hog if you're chasing two." Stay on track and focus 100 percent on the primary objective.

3. *Know when to quit.* There is such a thing as doing it right and then there is excess. Don't seek extreme results that are inappropriate for the task at hand. Don't strain for sounds that only dogs can hear. In annual report publishing projects, for example, I have known graphic designers who demand exacting color reproduction quality that would be unnoticeable to anyone but an experienced colorist with a magnifying glass yet would increase the cost of the job by an unacceptable amount. Know when enough is enough and when to let go.

■ *Rule 2. Make communications an obsession.* In business or personal life, you will rarely err on the side of overcommunicating. The gifted manager knows that good interpersonal communications isn't the oil that lubricates the business machine; it's the nuts and bolts that hold the whole thing together. Yet many people miss the mark because they either take communicating too lightly or substitute technology for it. True, there are more communication transmission systems available than ever before, but delivery systems that launch messages at lightning speed are worthless unless someone is using them effectively. The trigger is still the business manager who knows *what*, *when*, and *how* to get the point across—and to *whom*.

In the same way that your company uses effective external promotion to achieve your marketing objectives, you can employ effective internal (i.e., interpersonal) promotion to achieve your people-to-people management objectives. There is a whole universe of people with whom you need to communicate on a daily basis. That becomes second nature once you realize that everyone you work with inside the company is also your customer. Just as your external customers need your product or service, those folks all around you are your internal customers, and they also need something from you. They are the people who depend on you for information. They are also the people you depend on for information and for work to be done.

> Never underestimate the importance of communication.

Make it your priority to study and understand this customer and to realize that each one is unique. The astute manager knows that each person's motives are different and each works for a little different reward: It may be tangible (i.e., money), creative, status- and ego-driven, escapist, or social. Others work out of a sense of duty. The list goes on and on. And the motivation changes over time, so you have to stay tuned in and listen carefully to understand what makes a person tick at any given time. Then you can shape your message and communicate clearly with individuals in one-on-one situations, as well as deal with the information needs of the larger team.

The manager who is passionate about communicating follows these guidelines:

1. *Consider who needs to know what—and how and when they will receive the information.* Take personal responsibility for making it happen, whether you interface directly with your internal customers, send them notes, or have an up-to-date bulletin board, briefing system, or message center.

2. *Have a regularly scheduled meeting for your staff or any team that works closely together on an ongoing basis.* Have a set time and stick to it, even if it's a ten-minute meeting first thing each Monday morning. Breakfast or luncheon meetings are acceptable but are rarely as effective as a focused meeting dedicated only to the conduct of business. Keep it moving and keep it interactive, drawing out reports on key actions or anything of substance that affects the enterprise.

3. *Don't overlook others who may be outside the inner circle.* Keep the secretary and the receptionist and the loading dock worker informed as well. When giving recognition, be particularly aware of including all peripheral members of the team who may have played a part. (It pays to practice random acts of kindness, too, by recognizing someone who

doesn't expect it. A very successful manager made a lasting impression at our company's headquarters by often acknowledging the clerical, mail room, and telephone personnel. It opened a lot of doors and he received his messages and company news before anyone else.)

4. *If the team is large enough, maintain an active electronic or printed work schedule.* The schedule shows what projects and actions are in progress, who is doing what, and when action is due. (You can add a budget or cost column to track financial status as well.) Update the work schedule and review it with the team regularly.

5. *Keep your communications as positive as possible.* Seize the opportunity to lift the spirits of others while you are delivering operational information. Find something complimentary to say about that person or the work being done. If you need to give some constructive criticism, do it in a positive way that is intended to help that person grow and develop. Avoid knee-jerk negative responses such as, "Why did you do that?" or "That won't work." If you're asked a question and don't have the answer, it's okay to say "I don't know"—as long as you add, "But I'll find out."

6. *Be clear and specific in your words—and expect others to do the same.* When someone says the job will be done as soon as possible, should you expect it by noon tomorrow or next week? When someone tells you it will cost "slightly

more," does that mean 2 percent more or 20 percent more? In your business communications, express yourself in very specific terms and ask others to do likewise.

7. *Be sensitive to misinterpretation in your writing.* For example, beware of written correspondence and e-mail that you may take very casually but the recipient takes very seriously. Give each message a second reading to avoid misunderstanding.

8. *Be honest in your communications.* Don't say things that you can't back up. And don't fabricate excuses to cover your mistakes. It's better to follow Harry Truman's example of frankness. During his 1948 presidential campaign, Truman was cornered by a reporter with an accusatory question as to why he stated a certain position in one city but stated exactly the opposite in another speech a week later. The media snickered, expecting Truman to go into a thrash mode, but his immediate reply was, "I changed my mind." The assembled reporters, who were totally unaccustomed to hearing that kind of direct response from a politician, were left dumbfounded. It's all right to change your mind when new evidence comes to light, as long as you don't do it so often that you're labeled as indecisive.

■ *Rule 3. Don't take yourself too seriously.* Take your work seriously. Take your responsibilities seriously. But don't let the office become your entire life. Writer Margaret Fontey says, "The most important thing I have learned over the years is the difference between taking one's work seriously and taking one's self seriously. The first is imperative, and the second disastrous." Give your work your serious commitment and an honest effort—but not as if your life depended on it. Don't let your job turn you into a one-dimensional character who thinks of nothing but work. Sure, business is exciting and it's easy to get totally immersed in it—even to the point of working just for the sake of working. That's sad enough during your working career, but it becomes even sadder once you quit. Those who retire and then find themselves lost without their jobs are restless souls.

> ### Don't let your job become your life.

To avoid this addiction, you need to do a little self-analysis. Is all my energy going into the business? Do I spend all my time, at work or away, thinking about business problems? Am I shortchanging my family, and do I still have a family? Do I play golf and socialize, but only with businesspeople who talk about business? Is most of my reading about business? If I wake up in the middle of the night, do I immediately think about some business issue? Do I often stay awake the rest of the night wrestling with it?

Don't get alarmed if you've done some of these things some of the time. There are those critical times when you must devote 100 percent to an assignment, but don't make that the norm. Be careful that you're not letting your work become your entire life. Take a hard look at just how much your work permeates your daily life and how it may be crowding out your family, emotional, and spiritual life. In a blinding flash of the obvious, you may realize that it's time to regroup and regain your perspective.

Add a little variety to your life. Take time to relax away from the job, hopefully in some hobby or interest that has nothing to do with your profession. Take a vacation during which you leave the laptop at home and switch off concerns about what's going on back at the office. Don't do what some business colleagues do—save up all the business and trade publications they haven't read yet, so they can "catch up on reading while on vacation." Any psychologist would tell you that reading or talking about business issues, even in the most idyllic environment, adds stress to the tormented manager.

Condition yourself to accept periods of inactivity and "doing nothing" without guilt. Look at it as a time to recharge your batteries so you'll be fresher when you do go back to work. The vitality of Greece's golden days was attributed in part to the importance accorded leisure: time spent in rest and contemplation of eternal questions. Today's managers equate leisure with entertainment and think of leisure as time spent racing frantically to get to a theater or sports event to be entertained by someone else. That's desperation, not quiet contemplation.

Finally, don't ever think you're indispensable. To illustrate the latter, place your hand in a bucket of water. Now withdraw your hand and see the impression that is left. None, right? Managers would like to create the impression that they are indispensable, but no one is "fireproof." Just enjoy your business life, but remember that it is a means to an end and only part of your total persona.

A CODE OF CONDUCT STARTER LIST

We've just perused three examples of rules to live by. Think now about other guidelines you'd like to plug into your personal code of conduct. Here are a few other suggestions:

- Don't say things about someone behind his back that you wouldn't say to his face.
- Maintain absolute integrity in all things at all times.
- Never do anything that you'll be ashamed of later.
- Praise in public, criticize in private.
- Treat your word as your bond and keep every promise you make.
- Always be on time!
- Accept responsibility for your actions.
- Don't spend time trying to save nickels and dimes, or that's what you'll end up with—just a lot of nickels and dimes.
- Accept the fact that success is not final and failure is not fatal.
- Don't be afraid of making a mistake, but avoid costly ones and never repeat the same mistakes.
- When you need professional advice, get it from professionals, not from your friends.

Nobody Said It Was Easy

Building new value foundations is not easy, especially when your existing philosophical structure has already been in place for years. It's like a house with standing walls and a heavy roof that has served you reasonably well. How can you just change the foundation? Well, you might take a lesson from the Shakers of a century ago. When they added a floor to an existing structure, they just jacked it up and added the new level below—keeping the rest of the structure and roof intact. It can be done.

Now that you have decided on the overall attitudes that will govern your management life and the ethical foundation is in place, you will be able to address the other challenges of management that await you. Tragically, many managers with immense potential break down on the road to success because their view of morality is that it is an inconvenient obstacle, and just something to get around. Savvy managers, they think, are too smart to adhere to those rigid beliefs. For them I quote the smartest source I can think of, a mathematical physicist who said, "The most important human endeavor is the striving for morality in our actions. Our inner balance and even our very existence depends on it. Only morality in our actions can give beauty and dignity to life." Who am I to quarrel with Albert Einstein?

My personal belief is that a solid spiritual base also contributes significantly to many other life decisions. Some of the best advice I ever received came from a rabbi who led the invocation at a Cleveland business convention. "As we harness technology and reach into outer space," he prayed, "let us not lose sight of the inner space within each of us." That reminded me of the words of philosopher Immanuel Kant when he admitted that the two things that filled him with most wonder are "the starry heaven above me and the moral law within me." Managing yourself begins on the inside and in finding that moral law within you. Along the way, you may also prove to some skeptics that "business ethics" is not an oxymoron.

C H A P T E R

2

MANAGING GOALS AND OBJECTIVES

"Will you tell me, please, which way I ought to go from here?" asked Alice. "That depends a good deal on where you want to get to," said the cat.

—*ALICE IN WONDERLAND*

How can you hit a target if you don't have one? And don't kid yourself—just seeing the flag isn't going to tell you exactly how far you are from the green. An understanding of how all the pieces of the planning puzzle interconnect is a must for the productive manager! If you are deficient in planning, your sins will find you out.

This chapter could just as easily have been described as being about goal setting, management by objectives, planning development, measurable performance, strategic thinking, or even coordination. All would be partly correct, but all—including goals and objectives—are incomplete because all such terms are part of the ominous-sounding planning hierarchy. Such is the semantics thicket we encounter when we venture into the serious business of planning. Perhaps with a guide, we can find the paths, and even the shortcuts, that can make you a planning-proficient manager who sees targets clearly and hits them consistently.

A management consultant once visited a business that was in the throes of a long, lingering downward slide. "How many people work here?" he asked one of the downcast managers. "About half of them" was the sardonic reply. That response was not far from being right. The deeper the consultant dug, the more he discovered that the organization was in a near-comatose state. Employees were not working, or at least not working productively, and the whole business seemed to be sleepwalking. The most conspicuous sign the consultant noted, though, was the absence of goals and objectives—at nearly all levels. "A lot of your managers retired ten years ago," he told the interim CEO, "but they just haven't announced it." They had not received clear directions from above, and—in the absence of a clear mission and planning structure—they had not gone out on a limb to create many targets of their own. Without a planning structure and purposeful goals and objectives, a job is just a habit and the worker may still be working—but has forgotten why.

THE BUSINESS-PLANNING HIERARCHY

One reasonable piece of homespun advice is, "Don't get any more organized than you have to be." If you never get any more organized than this, you must at least put an understanding of certain planning essentials into your toolbox. I suggest a neatly packaged, bare-bones planning hierarchy that, from top down, includes the following elements:

Mission
Situation analysis
Goals
Objectives
Strategies
Tactics

Let me give you a last-minute disclaimer (and a little assurance) before you set out to conquer these planning definitions. Can you do a business plan without understanding the difference between goals and strategies? Sure you can, and precise definitions are expendable as long as you truly understand business and think strategically. I am only gift wrapping the process because I have found it to be a huge help in getting

---

Without a plan, a job is just a habit.

the logically related parts of the business machine firing in the proper sequence. I offer it in the same way I give advice to young writers: "You must know the rules before you begin to break them." I think you will benefit as a manager if you start out with a proper understanding of these six steps to planning success. After that, you can call them by whatever name suits you.

For simplicity's sake, we'll refrain from delving into goals-within-goals, strategic concepts, long- and short-range planning, and other turns in the road. Just get your head around this planning sequence and you can later get as loose or as sophisticated with it as you wish. Ready, begin!

Mission

The company has to begin with a vision, an organizational dream of what the future company should look like. (Perhaps the most dramatic example of a literal vision comes from Martin Luther King's "I have a dream" speech, which projected his vision of a nonracist America.)

The articulation of the company's vision is its mission statement, which explains the organization's purpose. Mission statements have their skeptics, but you can send them scattering with research data—the *Journal of Business Strategy*, for example, suggests that companies with mission statements are more likely to be profitable than those without. Companies with a mission statement increased shareholder equity to an average return of 16.1 percent versus 9.7 percent for those without one.

The mission statement establishes the company's future course: It tells us who we are, what we are, and what we strive to become. In a few words (actually the fewer the better) a mission statement can give a clear focus to the company, employees, customers, and investors. Henry Ford began his 1903 statement with eight words: "I will build a motorcar for the multitude." The mission statement should go on to enlarge the company's view of itself, with no pious platitudes.

Mission statements are valuable, though, *only if everyone in the company understands them*. At Beckman, we made a major investment of time in explaining the shared mission to all of our constituents, but particularly to employees. As a result, almost any employee you met in the hall was conversant with the mission, and many employees carried pocket cards that contained vision, mission, and values statements. To understand the company's purpose is to begin to internalize it in your daily duties.

It doesn't have to be elaborate, either. IBM's mission statement can be boiled down to three parts: respect for the individual—whether customer, employer, supplier, or investor; pursuit of excellence; and delivery of outstanding customer service.

Kinko's philosophy has no mention of being open twenty-four hours, but it does mention a very strong commitment to serving its customers in a timely manner. In Kinko's view, that means its employees being there anytime they're needed.

Part of Johnson & Johnson's mission statement says: "Our number-one commitment is to the doctors, nurses, patients, and families who rely on our products." When the company faced its famous Tylenol scare, that mission was tested and confirmed. Employees knew what to do and pulled bottles from the shelves. The CEO was up-front in his communications with the public. As a result, the company and the product even grew in stature as a result of the crisis.

(As Stephen Covey suggests in *The Seven Habits of Highly Effective People*, you can also create a personal mission statement for yourself or your family. You are, after all, the one person you can control, and you can apply the same thinking to determine where you're headed in life and what you seek to become.)

Situation Analysis

You can call this research or fact finding if you like, but it is the process of obtaining the necessary information you need to create the work plans ahead. A situation analysis tells us where we are now. It is an awareness of the environment in which we must compete. It warns us of the threats lurking in the tall grass, as well as the golden opportunities just around the bend. Without the situation analysis, you're just swinging at a piñata that you can't see.

A timesaving shortcut is the SWOT (or WOTS Up?) analysis that pinpoints:

Weaknesses
Opportunities
Threats
Strengths

Consider these four aspects of both your company's external and internal environment. External considerations include customers, competition, technology, and economic conditions; the internal environment encompasses management and employees within the company, your products and services, and support services. For example:

■ A strength in the internal picture could be the large installed base of your company's products within your customer establishments, and the strong awareness and sales coverage you have in the marketplace.

■ If you are doing business in the medical field, an external threat could be a change in the government's reimbursement policy to hospitals, or a technological breakthrough by an old or new competitor.

■ An opportunity exists externally in the fact that your target market is growing 11 percent annually; the company may also be able to offer attractive rental and lease programs for those customers who cannot make a large capital investment for the product.

■ An internal weakness would be if your company is having difficulty attracting qualified production personnel, has inadequate internal control systems, or has a poor collection record on receivables.

Toward the end of World War II, a high-level U.S. commander was hurriedly dispatched to a recently occupied enemy country with the assignment to set up a workable administration for this war-disrupted area. On the flight to his destination, the commander scribbled down an overall plan outline, based in part on the kind of questions in this situation survey. That simple handwritten outline successfully served as the conceptual base for a whole country's control structure. Try it on the business territory you're controlling!

Goals

By definition, a goal is a statement of broad direction or intent that is general and timeless and is not concerned with a particular achievement within a specific time period. Sound like anything else you've heard? That's because goals are used and misused to the point that any general direction, aim, or purpose can become a goal. Even management scribes talk about specific measurable goals when they mean objectives. (I warned you about the semantic hurdles.)

> A goal is timeless. It's a bridge between your company's mission and its objectives.

A goal is a bridge between the mission statement and the objectives of the enterprise. Similar to vision, a goal represents a desired future condition, but it is more specific than the former and less quantitative than the objective.

The time frame is long term. How long? A onetime president of Matsushita Electric Industrial, when asked if his company had long-range goals, responded affirmatively. Next question: "How long are your long-range goals?" Answer: "Two hundred and fifty years." Question: "What do you need to carry them out?" Answer: "Patience."

If done right, a goal will be timeless. The goal doesn't change, only the means of attaining it. As you stand on the tee of a long golf hole, your goal is to get the ball on the green and into the cup in the least possible number of strokes. Your intent is to hit the ball straight down the fairway and continue on toward the green. However, your errant tee shot slices into the rough and now you are faced with trees you hadn't counted on. The goal has not changed, but your approach, strategy, and the tools that you require change frequently as you pursue the goal.

The stated goal for my company was:

> To position Beckman as the acknowledged world leader in providing analytical chemistry laboratory systems, plus exceptional customer support, across the continuum from bioresearch to the diagnostics laboratory market.

In a nutshell, this goal depicts the desired aim, identifies the business opportunity, allows that both quality products and people services are needed, and correctly suggests that there is an important technology flow in the market from bioresearch activity to the medical end user. To merely say you intend to be a world leader is pie-in-the sky; if you can attach it to a defined market, then you have a target in your sights.

Objectives

It is illuminating to compare current-day business strategy with that of the first treatise on military strategy, *The Art of War*, written 2,400 years ago by Chinese General Sun Tzu. The parallels are quite striking and shouldn't be all that surprising, since strategy had its origins in warfare and the word originally meant "generalship."

Sun Tzu's first and foremost principle of strategy was the "principle of the objective." The principle advises that "every undertaking must have an objective." It goes on to specify that the objective must be clearly defined and that all activity must contribute to its accomplishment. No wonder that management guru Peter Drucker also listed setting objectives as the first of his five principles of management and conceived management by objectives (MBO) to further define the tasks required of the visionary manager.

An objective is a precise result to be achieved by a certain time. Now you see the distinction between goals and objectives more clearly. Hopefully, the six standards for an objective will also fall into place as neatly.

Six Standards for Defining an Objective

1. *Results.* An objective must be stated in terms of expected results, not in terms of activities. How many different things we're going to do is less important than the results we anticipate.

2. *Specifics.* An objective must be expressed in specific terms, not general ones. For example:

   ■ To increase sales by 20 percent

   ■ To reduce operating expense by $500,000

   ■ To decrease fiscal-year telephone expense 15 percent below the fiscal-year actual of $12,000

   Ideally, objectives should be additive and deal with improvements, not the status quo.

3. *Time Frame.* An objective must state the time within which results are to be obtained. This is usually stated

within the fiscal year or by the end of a given quarter. For example:

■ To increase sales volume in a territory by 40 percent in the coming year over the $2 million actual of the past year

■ To fully train three in-store salespeople on carpet and flooring products before the end of the second quarter

4. *Measurability.* An objective must be measurable and include the means for measuring accomplishment. Measure as quantitatively as possible. For example:

■ To increase our brand recognition in this category by 20 percent, from 16 percent to 19.2 percent, as measured by the industry's annual audit of brand recognition

■ To add 1,000 qualified prospects to the mailing list

5. *Criticality.* An objective should concern matters that are critical to business success and worthy of major attention. Don't waste time on the trivial. For example:

■ To meet the major ISO requirements that will enable our products to be marketed in the EEC

6. *Attainability.* An objective should be difficult to achieve yet attainable. It should not be too easy, nor should it be impossible and demotivating to those pursuing it. For example:

■ To meet or exceed the positive 1.5 to 3 percent quarter-to-quarter increases in sales volume of the past six consecutive quarters

Strategies

Now we're getting down to business. A strategy is simply a plan to achieve an objective. In the same way that objectives are the implementation necessary to achieve a goal, the strategy tells us what activities are necessary to reach the objective—and also serves as an acid test of how reasonable or unattainable that objective may be. If real constructive strategies can't be devised, then the objective must be reviewed and modified.

A strategy is a key link between the objectives we set and the development of detailed action plans (tactics) to carry them out. Strategies are specific methods. If the company's investment plan is to penetrate new markets rather than to hold and defend or harvest, and one of the operating unit's objectives for the next fiscal year is to gain an 8 percent share of market in the new area of food processing, then one marketing strategy may be to use trade shows to demonstrate a company commitment to this new market and to generate inquiries. That strategy then triggers necessary action to develop the appropriate display and select specific show opportunities.

Tactics

You guessed it: A tactic is a detailed program of specific activities and the means for implementing a planned strategy. Eureka! We've found the final link in the planning process and can now turn the dogs loose. Now we can assign specific responsibilities of personnel and schedule day-to-day action items. We can also call these our operating plans or programs. The loop is completed. Let the party begin!

The Whole Plan, and Nothing but the Plan

By way of review, here's the whole six-part sequence, beginning with the company's loftiest aspirations right on down to slogging it out at ground level:

Mission	Tells us what we are
Situation analysis	Tells us where we are right now

Goal	Tells us where we are going in the future
Objective	Tells us where we are going to go now
Strategy	Tells us how we are going to get there
Tactics	Tell us who does what and when

PRINCIPLES SUITABLE FOR THE FAMILY

While this book deals primarily with business management, I would be remiss if I didn't mention that you can apply some of the same thinking to personal and family planning. Here are some examples:

1. *Personal Planning and Goal Setting.* You might begin the same way I did, by asking yourself: Why am I working? What do I want to accomplish? If my work is a journey, will I know when I've reached my destination? The people you know who are most alive, regardless of age, probably have scratched out the answers to those questions for themselves.

   Most personal plans for a family (or career plans for an individual) are quite simple, and few are ever formally developed and recorded. Ordinarily, you will identify only a few goals and will likely have a short-term and long-term plan. Short-term personal goals may be simple ones: to lose ten pounds before summer, to learn a foreign language this year, to liquidate the mortgage on the house in five years. A longer-term goal may be to change jobs or careers, to relocate to a more desirable area, to retire at age sixty, or to begin planning for a second home.

2. *Family Five-Year Plans.* My wife and I have a more detailed written five-year plan that suggests our goals

and objectives over the next few years. The plan addresses finances, family, health and fitness, education, spiritual growth, social life, travel, and other life aspects. Each section begins by stating a long-term lifetime goal for that area. For personal travel, for example, our stated goal is as follows:

> To increase our knowledge of the world and expand our perspectives, we intend to visit five continents, traveling to the most distant destinations while health is not a factor and exploring nearer destinations in later years.

This is followed by a brief statement of prior accomplishments that highlights progress we've made to date. In the travel example, we cite action taken in acquiring a time-share vacation ownership and record destinations visited (and marked off our list). The important part of our plan is the last: our objectives for the current year and the next few years—listing places we intend to visit and trips to be planned.

Each year the plan rolls over and each section is updated, adding a new twelve month action plan and new specific objectives to the five-year outlook. In this plan, the goals seldom change but everything else does. The goals are our direction finders, and the objectives tell us what we have to do in order to realize them. It works for us—and reminds me why I'm working and what I'm working toward.

"A goal is just a dream with a deadline," author Marjorie Blanchard wrote. A media company president put it another way when he suggested, "Make a secret list of things you want to do before you check out. Put it in your billfold or purse and look at it from time to time. Examples might include a balloon ride, a river raft in Colorado, catching a five-pound bass, visiting the Taj Mahal, climbing the Great Wall, or snow skiing. Don't forget the little pleasures—a sunset, a walk along the beach, cold beer, or a kiss behind the ear. Develop a broad range of experiences. Don't define yourself solely by your job."

BUSINESS AND PERSONAL DIRECTION

In his book, *Innovation in Marketing*, Theodore Levitt recounts a story that deals with direction. Many years ago, Associate Supreme Court Justice Oliver Holmes once found himself on a train and unable to locate his ticket. While the conductor watched, he unsuccessfully foraged through all of his pockets. The conductor, who recognized him, finally said, "Justice Holmes, don't worry; you don't need the ticket. You'll probably find it after you get off the train, and I'm sure this company will trust you." The justice looked at him with some irritation and said, "My dear man, that's not the problem at all. The problem is not, where is my ticket? The problem is, where am I going?"

That's why managing personal and business goals and objectives is so important. If you don't know where you or your company is going, any road will take you there. To get where you want to be, though, it helps to have a route map and a timetable, as well as a ticket—a plan that includes the essential components you've just added to your memory bank. Empowered with this new wisdom, you can plan just about anything!

3

MANAGING
YOUR TIME

Dost thou love life? Then do not squander time, for
that's the stuff life is made of.

—*Benjamin Franklin*

Remember when the words "Time's up!" used to freeze you in position in classroom? For many managers, it still does. The specter of time running out is a constant threat in business. It doesn't have to be, though, and there are guaranteed ways to improve the yield in your workdays (and play days). Following just nine simple rules will give you better control over your time and make you wonder how you ever got along without them.

Time has been described as the most inelastic resource we have to manage. You cannot stretch it beyond the twenty-four hours in a day. You cannot expand it like you can staffing levels, plant space, or materials inventory. But you can control how you use it and increase the amount of work you get done in the available hours. You can also increase the odds that you're getting the most important things done. Everyone says "my time is valuable," but you can actually make your time more valuable than the next person's. This is more than just one-upsmanship, too, because if you can't manage time, it's unlikely that you can efficiently manage anything else.

There are nine time-tested principles of time management that I've employed that wear well and are easy to use. They permit you to make better use of the office time you have and even save more of your time for yourself, assuming you have other things you'd rather be doing. Here they are:

Nine Time-Tested Principles of Time Management

1. Establish priorities.
2. Welcome routines and procedures: They're your friends.

3. Transfer your monkeys to someone else's back:
   They're not your friends.　・
4. Delegate! Delegate! Delegate!
5. Manage incoming mail and phone calls.
6. Organize your paperwork and your space.
7. Use time in large chunks, when necessary.
8. Learn to say no.
9. Estimate your time needs.

How many times have you stood in awe of a neighbor or colleague who seemed to be juggling a dozen tasks and getting them all done as smoothly as clockwork. We all know people like that—a good worker who leaves a clean desk, manages the little league team, serves on the library's board of trustees, sings in the choir, works in the PTA, raises five kids, and still has time to jog every day and attend yoga classes. The eternal question is, "How do they do it?" The answers are tucked away in this chapter. Ready to get your time under control? Let's get started.

If you don't make a priority list, you may
not get anything done at all.

ESTABLISH PRIORITIES

You can't do everything at once. And if you don't begin with a priority list, you may not get anything done at all. Chances are that you will work at it hit-or-miss, invariably wasting more time than if you'd spent a few minutes up front for planning. Worse yet, you'll avoid the onerous jobs and only do those things you like to do, whether or not they are important.

What you are ultimately seeking is the answer to what has been called Lakein's question because it has been asked so often. It comes from Alan Lakein's book *How to Get Control of Your Time and Your Life*, and it goes like this: "What's the best use of my time right now?" Planning for the most important tasks will make a whale of a difference.

Admittedly, there are all kinds of planners and "to-do" lists floating around, electronic and otherwise, but there is no perfect solution—not when you're under constant pressure, involved in many activities simultaneously, on the ragged edge of one deadline or another, and scrambling to put out fires. But you can clear the smoke away by listing each day's priorities, in order of importance, identifying those things that must be done today. In so doing, you will also identify those things that can be done later, by someone else, or not at all. The important few are lifted above the trivial many.

It's an old moss-covered technique, but it never hurts to identify your ABC priorities in the list—with As as "must do" important and urgent items, Bs as "should do" important but not urgent items, and Cs as "could do" urgent but not important items. You'll find that you usually jump on A items because they are red hot and that you may spend more time on Cs than is necessary. Don't overlook the B tasks because they are important and, if ignored, will become urgent soon enough. (Of course, there are also a few nonessential Ds that should be either scratched off or handed off to someone else.)

A Classic Way to Prioritize Your Work

A Important & Urgent	B Important, Nonurgent
C Urgent, Nonimportant	D Nonurgent & Nonimportant

As tasks are completed, delete or cross them off your list. At the end of the day, the jobs that weren't completed are transferred to the next day's list and merged with new jobs. I've found that it not only works wonders in organizing your day, but you may wish to retain the data as a valuable work record and reference.

Here's what one company president has to say about setting priorities: "This simple technique has succeeded in organizing and ordering my working day and provides new peace of mind. The first thing I do on arriving at the plant each morning is to prepare a list of tasks to be done that day in order of importance, and I keep the list right in front of me so that the items bug me until they're crossed off."

WELCOME ROUTINES AND PROCEDURES

Some folks avoid routines and procedures like the plague. Little do they know that routines and procedures may turn out to be your best friends. They can sure save you a lot of time.

Routines = Unconscious Competence

Routines have gotten a bad rap. People talk about "just the same old routine" as if it were something painful. Yet champions in any field practice their techniques and movements over and over until they become routine. A professional golfer, for example, may repeat a physical action again and again, improving wherever possible, until it can be performed automatically without conscious effort.

That's how people learn to drive a car. You begin as a novice who is consciously incompetent, knowing that you don't know what to do. In time, you become consciously competent, knowing what you have to do to operate the vehicle, but still tethered to thinking very deliberately about each step. Finally, you have done it enough to become unconsciously competent, so you are able to drive without giving much thought to the sequence of steps involved. Driving becomes routine. Whatever your pursuit or business endeavor, it will be easier when you reach that competence level with sensible time-saving routines.

Procedures = Process-Oriented Thinking

While routines are habitual and unconscious in nature, you can also save time by reducing any series of repetitive steps to a procedure. Look at the process! If you're serious about managing time wisely, the thing you want to avoid is reinventing the wheel each time out of the gate. Analyze the tasks you do each day, particularly those with a number of steps involved, and begin to standardize those steps. Establish a logical flow.

The value of procedures can surface in even the most mundane tasks of everyday life, like washing the dishes. Did you receive instructions when you bought your dishwasher, or do you instinctively follow a system for loading a dishwasher? A neighbor, apparently with no such system, confided that she had just discovered that she could save several minutes a day with a procedure for loading her dishwasher. Previously, she had loaded dishes with no forethought, trying to fit plates and bowls on racks wherever she could. Since the same dishes were used regularly, she finally gravitated to a system allocating a specific area in the dishwasher for cups, bowls, glasses, small plates, large plates, and so on. She says she can now load quickly because she knows where each item will go (and how many items the space will accommodate). When the wash cycle is over, she can also unload and put away items much more quickly.

Whether it's quality control, mail handling, screening job applicants, or cleaning up after Thanksgiving dinner, using a procedure saves time and may, over time, become an unconscious and welcome routine.

TRANSFER YOUR MONKEYS TO SOMEONE ELSE'S BACK

Do you have too many monkeys on your back? I'm talking about responsibilities that you either assumed or let others put there for a free ride. How did they wind up on your back in the first place? Let me give you a quick example: You're walking down the hall on the way to a meeting when a subordinate approaches you. He has been given a daunting assignment to prepare a report on field sales activity for an upcoming meeting. He asks you a multifaceted question about the desired format for the report—amount of detail, time periods displayed, the need for information that may require additional input from the field offices. Because you're in a hurry and can't answer his questions on the spot, you say, "Let me look into it, and I'll get back to you." What has happened? The subordinate, who was carrying the monkey on his back, has gently transferred that primate to your back. He doesn't have to do anything until his boss (you) gets back to him with the information. Furthermore, you are the one who has to "look into it"—even perhaps make calls to the field, when that was your colleague's assignment. Now, repeat that scenario a dozen times a day, and you have become a leaning "tower of monkeys."

What should you have done? You should have told him to continue to march—to proceed with his assignment—using his own judgment. He should make whatever calls are needed and put together his own recommendation for the report's format and make an appointment—at your convenience—for you to review what he has accomplished (not the other way around, where he reviews what you have accomplished).

You get the idea. This is not to say that you will ever walk about monkey-free. But you will be blessed if you are only carrying the baggage that goes with your job. You will not become the dumping ground for everyone else's responsibilities. You will have saved an enormous amount of your valuable time, and you will have placed the monkeys where they belong.

DELEGATE! DELEGATE! DELEGATE!

Of all the foggy misconceptions to rise from the management swamp, perhaps the foggiest is delegation. It gets confused with work assignment or staff development, but it is rarely mentioned as the linchpin of time management.

Many folks shun the term because delegating sounds as if we're giving up some control. Nothing could be further from the truth. Effective delegation only gives you, the manager, more control over your time so that you can address more important priorities. If management, by definition, is "getting things done through people," then it necessitates delegation. Delegation is not getting other people to do your work, but giving other people the right to make decisions so that the work gets done.

> Delegation is the linchpin of time management—
> but it's hard work.

Why Delegation Becomes Difficult

Another reason some of the time management literature shies away from discussing delegation is that delegation is hard work, and it may not save time unless it's done properly. It can accomplish some other useful ends, but saving time may not be one of them. That's because up front you are going to have to invest some of your own time teaching, monitoring, and reviewing the work of others. At the beginning, it's tough work, and it isn't made any easier just because you have highly talented people. PepsiCo believes the secret of having good people is to "hire eagles, then teach them to fly in formation." But accepting instruction doesn't come easily to eagles. It is going to take some time to prepare people for delegation, but the rewards are worth it.

Assigning Work Isn't Delegating

Don't confuse delegation with work assignment. If you ask your assistant to type a letter you've written, you're not delegating, you're assigning. You're not giving up any control. You're not really saying "You're in charge." If, on the other hand, you gave that person the responsibility to create the letter for you and then sign it, you've successfully delegated a part of the task. If you sign it without reading it, you have not only delegated and given control to the assistant, but also demonstrated that when you said, "You're in charge," you had enough confidence in the person to back up the work without question. You have saved some of your time. You have delegated authority. Yet you're still responsible. Authority can be delegated—responsibility cannot.

The Gift to Yourself That Keeps on Giving

Here's the most important decision you can make regarding delegation: Delegate permanently to subordinates those activities that more logically belong with subordinates. This significant timesaver can be repeated over and over every day. You have appropriately taken one of your burdens and given it to someone else—permanently! After you've delegated a task or activity, don't look over the delegate's shoulder all the time. You may call it coaching or counsel, but it looks a lot like interference.

Passing Work Down the Line

Delegating is breaking off chunks of your own job and handing it to someone else—your delegate (who, in turn, should be allowed to break off pieces and hand them down the line). And why not? What you may have considered a small part of the job can be a really big deal to someone down the line. It represents a challenge and a well-deserved opportunity. Delegation is also an important development tool to prepare employees for increased responsibility later on.

Remember, though, that everyone down the line must also be given the information needed to do the job. To do her best, the delegate must understand the assignment and how it relates to the overall objective. When the delegate fails, the manager must accept the responsibility for a failure to inform, train, or motivate. It's also a matter of trust, in that you must trust others to do the job as well, or almost as well, as you would do it.

Don't Dawdle Over Delegation

Sure, you wonder sometimes why anyone would choose to delegate. Many managers delay making the move or simply say, "It's easier if I just do it myself." That may seem easy and convenient, but it's not sound logic. Focusing on the easy things is like the man who searched for his keys near the lamp post, not because that was where he lost them, but because that's where the light was best. In the long run, you will come to see that delegation makes good sense and will free you to do the more important management tasks that only you can do.

If it makes you feel any better, there's even a biblical precedent for delegation. In the Book of Numbers, Moses is complaining to the Lord about all the administrative tasks he has on his hands trying to lead the children of Israel. God dispenses some divine business advice, instructing Moses to select some competent elders and telling him, "I will take some of the spirit that is on you and put it on them; and they shall bear the burden of the people along with you so that you will not bear it all by yourself."

MANAGE INCOMING MAIL AND PHONE CALLS

Unless you are careful, you can fall into the trap of letting the telephone, the in-basket, and e-mail determine how your time is spent. They will dictate how much work you do and in what sequence. Management guru Peter Drucker says that businesspeople deceive themselves about the way they budget their time, believing that their time is well controlled and being spent productively while, in reality, much of it is wasted. Often time is squandered in exactly the areas we think we control best: business mail, e-mail, and the telephone.

To tighten your control over these time thieves, try these suggestions.

Consider Mail Time as Decision Time

Let's assume that you have already established priorities for what things you are going to do today, so you have a feel for how much time you can devote to incoming mail. Here are some techniques that work for me:

■ *Handle the mail once a day, and don't keep going back to it.* My office received regular mail twice a day, but I ordinarily saved the mail until four in the afternoon. After I felt I had accomplished most of what I had expected to do for that day, I used the mail to help plan what I would do tomorrow. You can build your schedule around a morning mail call just as easily. The point is, don't spend so much time waiting for mail and shuffling mail that it becomes the high point of your day.

Electronic mail is a slightly different problem. Since it can be monitored more easily and responded to immediately, you will want to access it more frequently or save, read, or respond as necessary to fill in holes in the workday.

■ *Try to handle each piece of paper only once.* Alec MacKenzie, author of *The Time Trap*, taught us the importance of "single handling" paper. Ask yourself, "What can I do with this piece of paper to make sure I never have to see it again?" (In actuality, a typical piece of paper is handled eight to ten times.)

Here's how to defuse the paper explosion: Separate the critical mail that requires higher-priority action, but make a decision on each piece of mail. Either take action on it, toss it, mark it for routing to someone else, or take a desired action and return it for filing. E-mail works the same way—either take action or delete it. If you want to save it for some reason, print and file if you maintain extensive paper files or store it in your computer.

■ *Have an assistant scan and sort mail, based on criteria you have established.* Many of the priority categories are similar to those you may use for projects on your daily to-do list. I have a "hot" (red) folder that contains personal memos (often from my boss) that require fairly immediate action and response. I have a second (yellow) folder for mail that is important but not urgent, and a third (white) folder for promotional mailings and other FYI mail. Set up your own color-coding system with whatever visual cues help you.

■ *Keep a yellow highlight marker at hand when you review the mail you will keep.* Highlight the key facts or action items. That way, if you must refer back to mail a second time, you can pick out the highlights in a hurry.

■ *Add some specificity to the outbox.* Have a multilayered box (or separate boxes) labeled for Action, Copy, File, or other categories of action required. Your assistant will appreciate it, and it will save you several follow-up questions.

Observe Phone Sense and Sensibility

Reach out and touch everyone, but do it in an efficient way. For example:

■ *Lump the small tasks.* Dr. Livingston said upon his return from Africa, "It wasn't the lions and tigers that got us, it was the gnats." Handling those harmless little calls can eat up your office time as easily as the large carnivores. If you have several phone calls to return, make them more efficiently at one sitting.

■ *Smile when picking up the phone.* The caller will hear it in your voice.

■ *Try to take a brief break between each call.* Take a few deep breaths, or have a drink of coffee to avoid getting tense. You can prevent the attitudinal residue from one event spilling over to the next. Your mind will be more focused and your judgment clearer.

■ *Be prepared!* Before you make that critical call—or even if you're expecting the call—get ready for it! Have any reference material you need spread out before you on the desk. Think about what you are going to say and maybe jot down a few brief points, including the questions you are going to need to have answered. Take an additional step by anticipating what responses you are likely to receive and sketch out a small decision tree to address a "yes" answer, a "no," or a "maybe." Where would each branch lead you? Anticipate what questions the other party may ask and what response is most appropriate on your part. Don't close without making your point, and—if a callback is needed—ask, "When is the best time to call back?"

■ *Set time limits, if possible.* Say, "I've only got about five minutes, but I wanted to let you know. . . ."

■ *Write it down.* If the call is important, take notes during the conversation, beginning at the top of a sheet with the caller's name and the time called. Write down any key points and any specific numbers, prices, dates, or times mentioned. (Believe me, you won't remember them if you don't write them down.) And write the notes on one sheet of paper. How many times have you later dug through the wastebasket to retrieve some marginal note you wrote on an envelope or newspaper during a conversation?

■ *Avoid speakerphones.* I don't use them and don't like to be on them. The exception is a conference call in which all parties know they are participating. Most people are uncomfortable discussing business issues when they have no idea who else is on the other end—or who may unexpectedly walk into that office during the call. I know it can be dangerous, because I have been there when privileged information went to the wrong ears.

■ *Know how to hang up.* Terminating a call should be the easiest thing in the world, but sometimes it isn't when a caller is both loquacious and tenacious. You can usually explain that you have to go to a meeting, have someone waiting, or must take another call. You can often set up a closing by firmly thanking the caller for the information and suggesting some later action. A simple but clear statement such as "Is there anything else we need to discuss?" can bring a conversation to a close. I often wrap up a rambling phone call by saying, "Well, I'd better let you get back to work now." Perhaps you have already devised some practical scheme to deal with this problem.

The most extreme method I've heard about was employed by a weak-willed service representative who couldn't seem to shut off the stubborn caller—so he just hung up on himself while he was talking. The caller's most reasonable conclusion was that it was a technical snafu, since it was the service rep who was cut off. (Don't try this if you're going to hang up while the other person is talking.) It seems to me that, at best, this is a dubious dodge that could only buy time for a more convenient callback at a later time.

Follow the "kindergarten model"
to organize your office.

ORGANIZE YOUR PAPERWORK AND YOUR SPACE

Not surprisingly, if you organize your space, you'll be halfway to organizing your paperwork. The secret is what is today called the "kindergarten model of organization." My wife is an elementary and kindergarten schoolteacher, and she has always insisted on her classroom space being organized functionally. The space is allocated by the activity to be performed there. There is a reading area where you'll find the book basket and library, an area set aside for music, another for arts and crafts, a snack shop, and one for the kids' coats and sweaters. The result is that children know where to go for each type of activity, that they are able to concentrate on only one activity at a time, that all the materials they need are stored and readily accessible in that area, and that they have a visual roadmap for the whole area. Even if it's the child's first time in the room, it's easy to figure out what to do and where to go.

You can organize your office or service area following the same model.

- ■ *Decide upon the overall scope of activity to be performed within this space.* Does it make sense? Should mailing activities actually be done here or in another area? Should supplies storage occupy this prime work space?

- ■ *Plan your areas.* What is the best location for my office and desk; the computer; the files; the library and reference materials; clerical, stationery, and other supplies; mailing or shipping materials; copy machine; meeting space; coffee room? These may be actual rooms or just space set aside for that particular activity. Does office form follow function? Is there a logical flow, or is the file cabinet clear across the room from the people who'll be regularly accessing it?

- ■ *Consider the associated furniture and supplies required for each section.* How much furniture is needed and exactly how should it be positioned? Remember that frequency of use should determine accessibility. (The same principle applies in cleaning up your desk: Sort and group those items that go together or are used together. Personal items, newspapers, and supplies don't belong in the middle of your work area.)

- ■ *Configure your office to fit your style.* If you like to have a lot of meetings in your office, allow for ample seating. If you need a work space for assembling or sorting, set aside a good surface for that purpose. If you're tempted to be a pack rat and store stuff away for later action, by all means avoid a credenza that will become an instant storage locker. Decide, too, upon desk position. Do you prefer to face the door so you can see what's going on around you, or with your back to the door to discourage interruptions?

■ *Implement and eliminate.* Carry out the plan, and eliminate everything that doesn't belong. Get rid of old files and paperwork. Toss old directories, magazines, and mailings. Most companies have a records retention policy as to how long to keep certain classes of materials. You have no such constraints on your personal paper collections, though, so round-file those stacks of old trade journals and business papers. The information is probably out of date and you won't get back to them, anyway. (When in doubt, save tax or legal papers.) If you want to save a particular magazine article, tear it out, but don't save the whole magazine.

How worthwhile is it to have your office and desk in order? *The Wall Street Journal* reports that the average U.S. executive wastes six weeks per year searching for missing information in messy desks and files. Would you like to reclaim those six weeks? With your office organized, your work space in order, and your desk under control, you'll have a handle on time management you never thought possible.

USE TIME IN LARGE CHUNKS, WHEN NECESSARY

You can accomplish many important things with a relatively small share of your total working time—if you can consolidate it in fairly large time segments. Sounds impossible? You can control more time than you think, but you have to be ruthless with your time schedule if you hope to save uninterrupted time for those priority projects. Suppose, for instance, that you have an important report to prepare that requires four hours. You're much better off to block out one morning for this job than to peck away at it thirty minutes at a time, twice a day, for four days. Actually, it would take far longer because you will need fifteen or twenty minutes in each instance just to get your papers out and your attention focused.

Far too many businesspeople have been led to believe that the only uninterrupted segments of time are found working late at the office or at home. If their workday was better organized, they might unshackle themselves from after-hours schedules or the burden of carrying home a load of office work each night.

I've found that the way to create large time blocks is to schedule them and protect them fiercely. Make an appointment with yourself. Treat that time just as if you were out of the office. Write it in your calendar and block off those hours. Close the door. Don't allow interruptions, and don't interrupt yourself by handling any other small issues. If the office environment is so fraught with interruptions that you can't concentrate, try an empty office or meeting room as an option. (When hounded with office interruptions, one technical writer used to take refuge in a nearby public library.)

LEARN TO SAY NO

Say no when you mean "no"! You will save countless hours and a lot of grief. I know it's awkward for people who have been taught to be polite and accommodating, but consider the alternative. Saying "yes" means you will be saddled with responsibilities and appointments that you don't want, will try to get out of, and won't handle in a way befitting your ability. Most executives have no trouble saying no to a telephone marketer, but are tongue-tied when it comes to turning down a business associate who asks a favor or solicits their presence at a fund-raising dinner. Learn to say no more often. Most people will respect you for it.

When you must say no, it's important that you have a reason even though you don't have to give it. Don't cop out over some trivial reason, but do accept the fact that your time is important! If you can't give a full commitment, then you should respond by saying, "You know that I would like to help you out, but I would be breaking my own rule: I just won't take on something unless I can give it 100 percent. Right now I have too many other priorities to do it justice, and that wouldn't be fair to either of us." Explain that other things must be taken care of first and add, "I'm sure you understand. I wouldn't expect you to accept anything less than a total effort, but I'm flattered you asked."

ESTIMATE YOUR TIME NEEDS

One of the original Murphy's Law corollaries is this: Everything takes longer than you think it will. Knowing that eternal truth, why don't we allow for it? Perhaps because we live in a world with so many controlled segments that we have become inept at handling the variables. We usually don't know exactly how long a given project will take, how many interruptions we may have, how long we will have to wait for input or approvals from others, and what delays or revisions may be in store for us.

We can, however, learn to estimate our time by practicing a few simple things. And, like the man who was surprised to learn that he had been talking prose all his life, you may find that you've been going through these motions without knowing it.

Begin with the end in sight, and work backward. This is not rocket science. Time scheduling is something you already do, though you may be making one big guess instead of making several small and more specific guesses. If you're having trouble with travel planning, for instance, try this exercise: If your flight leaves at 10:00 A.M., start there and work backward to calculate what time you need to be at the airport and how much time you should allow for check-in. Next, ask how much travel time you need to get to the airport, allowing for anticipated traffic delays and unanticipated slowdowns, and to get parked (if you are driving). How much time do you need to complete packing and be ready for departure (without leaving anything important behind, like reading glasses)? How much time to get dressed, and how much time to bathe? At the end of this mental countdown, you will have a pretty good idea of the amount of total time needed, and that's a signal as to the exact time you need to start. It may sound tedious, but it will take less than a minute to complete this exercise. Besides, wouldn't you rather begin your trip fresh and in control? If you're like me, you will not only go through this simple process, but will probably add a few minutes' "cushion" as well. So you're a few minutes early. That's not wasted time if you have your laptop, something readily available to read, or a few minutes to review your schedule for the day.

The board chairman and CEO at Beckman Coulter, Lou Rosso, was a terrific guy but a terror when it came to travel. He arrived at airports at the very last minute, cool and collected, while his travel party sweated bullets. "He doesn't have ulcers," one associate said, "but he's a carrier." He was there when he had to be, but often cut it very close. When our company merged with SmithKline in 1982 (a merger that later ended in 1989), the availability of the SmithKline jet helped alleviate the angst of top executives stewing over those commercial flight schedules.

Good time estimating is a learned skill. Practice it often, and be aware of whether you're repeatedly underestimating or overestimating. Most people underestimate the time required, or heed another whimsical Murphy's Law corollary: The real deadline is one week after the original deadline. The first time you discover that the real deadline was the original deadline, you (and your career) may be taking on water. Underestimating the task can also fool you into thinking you can do it in your spare time when in reality you have no spare time. (As Yogi Berra said, "If you can't get it done in twenty-four hours, you've got to work nights.")

Likewise, there is a danger in overestimating the time required, which can eventually lead to squandered time. A more dangerous result of overestimating is that you become intimidated with the imposing task and either say, "It's more than we can handle," or procrastinate starting on it altogether. If you feel a task is too big, apply the familiar "Swiss cheese approach" and poke holes in it. Break it up into smaller assignments, but start somewhere. This isn't something fresh out of today's textbooks. No less than Mark Twain said, "The secret of getting ahead is getting started." "Do it now" is still the best advice you may ever get.

TOO MUCH OF A GOOD THING?

Can you practice time management to a fault—that is, to the point where it is a detriment to the business? Probably not, unless you reach a point of paralysis from analysis and overexamination, like the gardener who keeps pulling up the flowers and looking at the roots to see if they're growing. But well-meaning people can, and do, occasionally create other unexpected problems in their efforts to save time. I recall a division manager who was assigned from California to revive a troubled division near Chicago. Since it was not a longtime or permanent assignment, the manager maintained his home and family on the West Coast and commuted weekly. That's the good news. The bad news was that this energetic executive, unattached to home and family responsibilities, had all his time for business! That led to a marathon of business dinners, late-night meetings, and early morning working breakfasts. In his mind, he was saving employees' time by making his time available to them at all hours. The truth is that it wreaked havoc on the personal and family life of the folks who lived there. In managing your time wisely, be sensitive to what effect it may have—good or bad—on others. The early bird gets the worm, but that's not a fortuitous event for the worm.

C H A P T E R

4

MANAGING YOUR BOSS

Don't think of me as the Boss, just think of me
as a friend who's always right.

—*Anonymous*

Bosses . . . you gotta love 'em! It's easy to do when you're working for a good one, but troublesome when you're in league with a marginal one. There are more rewarding things to do than jousting with the bully boss; prodding the cautious boss; or providing damage control for the impressionable, impulsive boss. But don't be surprised to learn that nearly all bosses can be managed, and a lot easier than you ever thought possible.

When Peter Drucker defined the art of management as "getting things done through people," he didn't specify that those people are your subordinates. They're not. Some are your peers, and one is your boss. All things considered, managing the boss is the most critical single task on your agenda because you can perform only to the extent to which a boss allows you to become effective. You need to manage the boss to increase your personal effectiveness and to prevent your boss, knowingly or unknowingly, from blocking your progress or restricting you in the accomplishment of your objectives.

Managing the boss is more than just avoiding a negative hit. You need to manage the boss because of the benefits that await you. It's squarely in your own self-interest. Each manager depends on a superior for support, understanding, review of performance, guidance, and ultimate success. It's only in the movies that a person succeeds because the boss is an incompetent buffoon. Fact is, your chances of success are much greater with an intelligent, achieving boss than with an incompetent one. In a way, the superior depends on the subordinate as much as the subordinate depends on the superior, and it is to your advantage to help the boss perform effectively. Providing that help in a nonthreatening way, however, is like walking through a minefield. Here are a few lessons I've learned that may help you tiptoe through it safely.

> Your chances of success are much greater with an intelligent, achieving boss than with an incompetent one.

BAIL OUT ON THE CRAZY BOSS

Before we map out any strategies for dealing with a boss, let's first eliminate the lunatic fringe. Most bosses, like most people, are upright, motivated, and fairly sensible citizens. Occasionally, however, you may encounter a boss who is—in a word—incorrigible. I would suspect that this happens less than 5 percent of the time, but it can happen. If that is the case and you see no immediate resolution in sight, then you should cut your losses and get out. I am not a believer in undermining a boss or working to expose someone's failures. I think that's a negative, draining enterprise that takes far too much of your time—time that should be spent building your career and not tearing down another's. It can make you bitter, too. You may, at best, end up like a grizzled old veteran who proudly told me, "I don't have an enemy in the world. I've outlived all the sons of bitches!"

EXPECT JERKS WITH QUIRKS

Be prepared to work for a jerk every now and then, but don't get all tied up in knots because a boss has a few quirks and foibles. Some of those character deficiencies, while unsuitable in private life, may seem particularly well suited for this boss's business career. You can cope with these traits and maybe even turn them to your advantage. Yes, there's hope for the weak boss who couldn't lead a group in silent prayer. There's hope for the bully who seems bereft of any sensitivity or kindness. There's hope even for the selfish boss who says, in effect, "I like your idea; I'm glad I thought of it."

Instead of sinking into depression, take heart. In the next few pages you will find some tips to help you manage a boss who's too tough to overlook, but too valuable to desert.

Steps in Managing the Dysfunctional but Operational Boss

Learn All You Can About the Boss

No, I don't mean engage in some sort of espionage. Just the things that might help you flesh out the whole character of this individual in your mind—schooling, family, interests, vacation habits. After that, look a little closer at the boss's business style.

- *Is this person a reader or a listener?* Dwight Eisenhower was a reader—"Leave me the report, and then talk to me later." Jack Kennedy was more of a listener—"Let's discuss this, and then leave me a summary." Obviously, if you have a boss who won't read anything, you don't want to waste your time preparing a long written report that's going nowhere.

- *Is the boss a morning person or an afternoon person?* People usually have a certain time they like to read the mail, check their e-mail, make phone calls. Observe when your boss is definitely not accessible and when he or she is most open and approachable. (I've known a boss or two who was most approachable even after normal business hours—when things have settled down a bit.)

Lead by Being a Good Follower

Before you can manage the boss, you must establish trust by being a good follower. I don't mean the meek corporate sheep who gets sheared every day, but a dynamic and proactive subordinate who can produce a spirit of win-win when dealing with the boss, someone who has built up the personal capital to challenge the boss's ideas in a respectful way (not behind the boss's back). Here are a few techniques:

- *Let the boss know what's going on.* It's the insecure manager who keeps the boss in the dark. Secure managers communicate openly and take responsibility for their actions.
- *Respect the boss's position.* Like the "office of the presidency" you should respect the position even though you may not agree with its holder or her way of doing things. Evaluate performance by the results, not the technique. You can learn a lot from the boss, even when the tuition cost is high.
- *Ask the boss:* "What is it that I do or my people do that helps you do your job, and how could we do that better?" Periodically repeat the same question in different ways. (Share the input with your staff as well.)
- *Let the boss know what can be expected from you.* Prove that you are not afraid of work and that you will follow through on whatever assignment you accept. What do bosses hate and love? They hate surprises. The five words they love to hear most are "I'll take care of it."

MANAGING THREE TYPES OF DIFFICULT BOSSES

The Bully

The authoritarian manages by fear and coercion, controlling from the top down and seldom (if ever) sharing with others in the decision-making process, since the authoritarian is generally insensitive to others' feelings. This is a style that worked for this person on the playground or at some earlier time in life, so he has stuck with it. It is perhaps not as visible in the boardroom as it is among high-profile coaches or managers—think Woody Hayes, Bobby Knight, or George Steinbrenner—but there is ample bully management in business as well.

Let me give you a prototypical example of a bully manager, one who was soft at the core but loved to intimidate. Mr. Big had all the tools for it, too: He was a huge, 300-pound man—a former University of Oklahoma football lineman—who had slogged his way to a position as the corporation's chief operating officer. It would not have been hard to believe him if he said, "I could squash you like a bug."

It was also apparent that Mr. Big liked to test people. In our company's corporate structure, for example, the trade show responsibility resided at the corporate level under my control and provided exhibit services to all the operating divisions. It was a multimillion dollar activity and spanned some forty trade shows per year—something that obviously required professional supervision and tight control.

In a testing mode, Mr. Big would approach me and say something like, "I've been talking to the divisions and we're going to give them the trade show responsibility." This happened to be patently untrue and, even if it were true, would not have been the end of the world. It was an important function, though, and one that greatly affected key markets and company investment.

Having been the target of several previous "sky is falling" scenarios from Mr. Big, I could identify the trade show example as just another test. Rather than be unnerved by the threat, I was able to seize upon the opportunity it provided to demonstrate a strong commitment to the organizational issues involved. I told him that this was not something he wanted to do, reminded him of the diffused image problems under the old system and pointed out the economies in using one flexible exhibit system for varied applications. I also stated that the ability to control and monitor our exhibit investment at the corporate level (his level) was a good thing for him. Whenever he had questions, I told him, he could get answers from one source (me) rather than from many different sources buried in the far-flung divisions.

Besides providing a useful review for my superior, I had managed the boss without stepping on a mine. His intimidating questions were no longer a problem, but an opportunity. Over time, his threats and tests became a kind of inside joke with me, and when it became clear that they were not generating the scare that he originally intended, he stopped them. (He used them on other managers, though, and probably gained a useful insight on which ones broke into a sweat and which caved in without offering opposition.) Later on, this particular bully boss even became a valuable ally and invisible shield in other company conflicts—all of which goes to show that when you're out on the playground, it's not all bad to have the bully on your side.

The Cautious Boss

This is not the insecure boss, dogged by paranoia. The cautious boss is confident, knows full well what she is about, and probably knows her job well. She just wants to make sure she is doing the right thing and consequently agonizes over decisions (and may even experience some remorse even after she makes them). The cautious boss probably read an old management text that suggested, "Never make a decision until you have to." That advice was intended to discourage snap decisions—to help managers adequately plan decisions so they don't have to retreat from them later on—not to bog down the process entirely.

If you think a cautious boss is difficult during normal times, wait until a crisis comes along. When the valve must be shut off and damage control initiated and every minute is critical, you can't afford to be stymied with an uncertain decision-making process. Fortunately, the cautious boss is redeemable and you can be an agent of this redemption.

> You can help a cautious boss make decisions.

Whatever the issue, the cautious boss can be redirected if she will make tentative decisions in advance, thereby avoiding the feeling that she's being rushed into an irrevocable final decision before it's necessary. You can help the cautious boss to consider alternatives in advance by drawing up a tentative game plan that provides some broad and flexible directions but leaves plenty of options open. When a decision is imminent, you provide the cautious boss with elements of the provisional game plan for your area of responsibility—pieces of the total plan that might suggest other things that could be added to flesh it out. Then, when the balloon goes up, the boss won't have to start the entire planning process from ground zero. She will already have some structure and options from which to choose. (If she is not amenable to your assistance, you will at least have anticipated many of the actions necessary to protect your own territory.)

You can assist in other ways, too, since your earlier analysis will have answered questions about the boss's strengths and weaknesses. Ask yourself: Why is the boss cautious? What are the areas in which she seems to entertain self-doubt? Are these areas where you can support and supplement her capabilities? If she has good ideas, for instance, but has difficulty organizing the facts and figures to support her ideas, perhaps you can play a stronger role in preparing the financial analysis that will move them forward.

CASE STUDY:

THE FUTURE IS NOW

Let me give you an actual example of successful management of this genre of executive—and how a sales and service manager whom we'll call Hal elicited an important decision from "CB," the cautious boss of an important business group.

CB, our group manager, is a good executive and is noted for her intellect and participative style of management. She is unquestionably one of the bright lights in the company and—although not aversive to risk taking—prefers to move slowly and at a velocity inversely related to the magnitude of the decision.

Hal, on the other hand, is a promoted sales manager from the field and is accustomed to moving quickly. He knows that the proposal he has in mind, one that entails a restructure of the field sales and service force, will encounter resistance from CB. Hal has thought about the proposal long and hard and is convinced that it is in the company's best interests to make the change quickly. Being fair and open-minded, he has mentally placed himself in CB's shoes and considered what her possible concerns may be. One large perceived risk is that this action may disrupt sales at a time when the company is approaching a major new product introduction. Any softening of sales now could affect the company's earnings and stature with the financial community. Hal suspects that even if the proposal passes the first hurdle, CB will want to exercise caution and implement the change in stages over a long period of time.

Taking all the pros and cons into consideration, Hal proceeds with a presentation to CB. But he pulls a rabbit out of his hat at the beginning of the presentation, not at the end. As he begins the discussion, Hal says that this is a proposal he is recommending for implementation two years from now. Then he moves skillfully through each point, answering and defusing possible objections that CB might raise and getting agreement from CB on each point. CB is an interested and participative listener. At the conclusion, Hal asks CB if she concurs with the thinking. CB, who has in principle bought each point throughout the meeting, firmly says "Yes." Then Hal applies the close: "Well, if it makes sense to do it two years from now, why don't we just do it two months from now?" The doors have snapped shut and CB is caught.

How did Hal manage the cautious boss? He disarmed the boss with the statement indicating that this was a plan for sometime in the future. CB relaxed and opened up to the logic. Because CB thought there was no looming decision to make, she concentrated on the positive benefits that Hal was unfolding and embraced it as a sound plan—rather than looking for flaws and building objections. This technique, which gives the illusion of a nonthreatening deferred action, lets the manager ease the boss into the decision-making process. It can be applied in many ways with the insecure and guarded boss who is reluctant to take the big step.

The Impressionable Boss

The only reason the impressionable boss makes the dysfunctional list is that he has no rudder. He wants to do the right thing, but when he is buffeted by the storm, he is repeatedly blown off course. "Keep your bow into the wind" has no meaning for him. He can be managed, but it will be a full-time job.

He is deficient in two dimensions: space and time. The space refers to the Olympian leaps he makes in jumping to conclusions. If he sees a customer and is told that our prices are too high, he comes back to the office railing about how we are pricing ourselves out of the market. Never mind that 85 percent of any company's customers will always report that prices are too high. Within the boss's mind, he can easily reach conclusions and stretch what one person says to cover the entire universe of buyers.

The time element means that his opinion on any issue depends on his most recent contact. He may hold fast to one opinion in the morning, have a luncheon meeting, flip-flop, and come back with a totally different point of view in the afternoon. Like the Pillsbury Doughboy, he is soft and pliable when given the slightest push, and you can only hope that you are the last person to see him before he makes a critical decision that is going to affect you and your staff.

I recall a marketing executive in our company's medical group who was an impressionable boss. He was told by one of our salespeople that what we needed to do was to put a high-quality binder containing all of our product literature into the hands of every hospital administrator in the country. (It could have been worse and been every hospital administrator in the world.) The suggestion sounded good to the boss. After all, it came from an experienced salesperson. This boss, being both impressionable and impetuous, was ready to launch the project immediately.

After he laid the idea on my doorstep, we conducted some research among hospital administrators and found that they had little interest in receiving a fat binder of catalogs. They were not the primary product specifier anyway, and the effect in the marketplace would have been hardly a ripple. However, as I pointed out to this boss, the financial impact within our company from a project of this scope would have been devastating. The expense of creating 8,000 binders, loading them with dozens of expensive brochures, and distributing them to administrators would have gutted our marketing communications budget. Besides being nonproductive, the binders would become obsolete almost immediately as new bulletins came through the pipeline. Who would have kept the books up to date? This and other questions were never asked. It's disturbing to consider how many overeager bosses are committing company dollars today, confident of their information sources and sure of their judgment, without doing the homework first!

Managing the impressionable boss requires a lot of contact to protect the boss from himself or herself. And it entails building trust so that the boss can accept input from others without making binding commitments, and defer action on a proposal until after it is reviewed with a trusted professional within the appropriate area of expertise. You need to call a time-out when things get out of control. Once you've coexisted with an impulsive, "ready, fire, aim" boss, you may even yearn to return to a cautious boss.

OTHER ASPECTS OF MANAGING MANAGERS

Matrix Management: The Marriage Made in Hell

"This is impossible," my friend in personnel said. "You know what's worse than having a boss—having two bosses!" I knew what he meant: multiple reporting relationships. Welcome to the world of matrix management, an organizational system not uncommon in multidivision technical companies, particularly in certain specialized departments such as legal, communications, and human resources. The idea is that you are in a particular corporate department and report administratively to its director, but you are also assigned full-time to an operating division and report functionally to its appropriate manager. You probably reside at the division as well. The ruling logic is that you are trained and evaluated by the corporate folks who are proficient in your specialty, but you apply your skills on behalf of the divisional customer. Ordinarily, the corporate boss is responsible for your performance review and salary action, but in consultation with the divisional bosses you're serving day to day.

Sound confusing? It can be. Sounds like it can put a strain on communications? It does. But it isn't something you haven't experienced before. You need only rewind to your childhood for the most classic example of all: parenting. You had a matrix system in your home with two bosses—each responsible for certain kinds of decisions. You went to your mother for some decisions and to your father for others. Like most kids, you probably played one against the other from time to time. Remember the hassles of getting the family car when you were a teenage driver? If the parents had faulty communications, that gave the child great opportunity to do mischief.

Much the same is true in matrix management within the company. If the two key bosses in the matrix do not communicate well or have conflicting goals, you may be caught between a hard place and another hard place. Opportunistic managers or staff will take great advantage of the seams between the two managers' governance. The supplicant can easily get approvals from one of their bosses based on misinformation about what the other boss wants. Often, the two matrix bosses go out of their way not to encroach on each other's domain, and the opportunist has license to work both sides of the street.

I am not fond of matrix management, although I can see, as in the parenting example, that it is sometimes a necessary alternative. Management expert Louis Allen included the principle of multiple reporting relationships in his famous principles of management with this terse description: "The more people to whom an individual reports, the more difficult it is to maintain accountability for results." Enough said.

When you report to two managers and your back is against the wall, you may do well to also remember Brintnall's Law, a relative of Murphy's Law: If you are given two contradictory orders, obey them both.

Don't Mistake Strength for Bullying

A strong, assertive manager, male or female, is not a bully. As a matter of fact, we expect bosses to display strength and a certain command presence. This is more basic than even the foundations of business and is displayed in a very visible, and sometimes entertaining, way within groups of primates. A group of chimps, for example, is typically governed by a dominant male—sometimes with a strong and loyal assistant as second in command. The degree to which the group is a harmonious unit is determined by how much respect they have for the boss. Groups that have a strong boss (who is seldom ever challenged) may be playful, but they are calm as they go about their daily activities. The young get into mischief but know what their limits are. The boss does not bully or harass members of the group, but they clearly know who's boss. Another, similar group with a weak or aging leader displays the opposite behavior. There are frequent challenges, agitation and screaming among its members, constant fighting, and unruly young running about.

> A strong boss often leads to a harmonious, stress-free workplace.

It may be quite a stretch from primates to pinstriped suits, but the group that has a strong, nonharassing boss and knows without question who is in charge can expect a happy and relatively stress-free workplace.

CASE STUDY:

THE STUDENT SHALL BECOME THE TEACHER

Bob, a young, newly appointed advertising manager, was on the way to the marketing manager's office to face his first management challenge of the new assignment. He had been summoned by the boss to discuss a budget review (a euphemism for a budget cut; bosses don't invite you over to discuss a budget increase). Bob's boss, Hank, was a tough marketing man, promoted from the field, but he was also open-minded and considerate. That was evident when Hank welcomed him into his office and carefully explained the financial predicament the operating unit faced. Part of the problem could have been foreseen, because budget cuts in this division were as predictable as the seasons. Each fiscal year burst forth in July with high hopes and healthy budgets. The first economic cold blast of fall, though, sent ripples through the accounting department and into the controller's office. The news was telegraphed to the department heads to trim budgets. (Some department heads hedged their budgets with as much cushion as possible in anticipation of the end-of-year cutbacks. Bob, unfortunately, had inherited a budget that was lean to begin with.)

Hank identified several red flags that had precipitated the cutting: a missed sales forecast, delays in the introduction of a major new product, behind-schedule recruitment of salespeople in the Northeast, among other factors. Then he dropped the other shoe. "It looks like we need about $100,000 from the ad department." This represented a significant part of Bob's total budget.

Bob had several options before him. The typical response would have been to say, "Okay, Hank, I'll go back to my office and rework the budget. I'll have it for you this afternoon." But Bob saw another opportunity that capitalized on his newness in the job—and Hank's patience. "Hank," he said, "since this is pretty new to me, I wonder if you could spare a few minutes to walk through this budget. It would help me to know what items are viewed as highest priority with you and the marketing objectives." Hank was willing, so they began reading through the budget, item by item.

One thing that became evident immediately was that the budget had been very well constructed. Every chunk of money was tied to a specific objective and had been estimated fairly. That added considerable gravity to the decisions. The trade-off became not how much to cut back, but which objectives to abandon. (The other methodology would have been to "lean down" *all* the budget. However, like leaning a fuel mixture, you soon reach the point at which the engine will no longer run.)

As each budget item (and objective) was addressed, Bob remained reserved, discussing each in an unbiased way and letting Hank volunteer his opinion. What had emerged, though, was that Hank had become the defender. Give up the planned brochure on the new product? Not on your life. "We've got to have it when the product is released, and you'll need to start on it right away." Cut back on sales aids and application data? No way. "We can't have sales troops in the field without ammunition!" Budget item after item was confirmed as absolutely necessary by the boss. Only one major expense was in jeopardy—the exhibit at the big trade show.

Hank had momentarily lapsed into an accounting mode and tried vainly to look only at cost—not effect. "We could save a bundle if we dropped out of that show this year," he mused, "including all the travel cost in my marketing budget." That's when Bob played his emotional card. He knew that although Hank had come from field sales, he was never very far from it mentally. He also knew that Hank was ferociously competitive and took the marketing battle with the number-one competitor very personally. On earlier occasions, Bob had observed how Hank could raise his blood pressure simply by discussing how the competition was trying "to eat our lunch" and "keep our kids from having a decent college education."

Bob might have countered a trade show cut by giving a rational expense analysis and detailing the penalties that would incur from show management at this late date and the effect a year's absence would have on the company's ability to get a prime space assignment in future shows. But he catered to Hank's competitive nature instead. "Well, there would certainly be a celebration at you-know-where," Bob said. "They'd love to have the field to themselves, and can you imagine the rumors they'd start? Without a booth, we'd also be handicapped in attracting and talking to prospects for those sales jobs you want to fill in the Northeast." Bob would have continued, but an animated Hank interrupted with some suggestions on how to make the booth more effective and exhibit plans for the new product introduction.

When Bob left Hank's office from his budget review session, his budget was not only intact but—surprise, surprise—had been augmented by $30,000 to strengthen certain areas! In addition, Hank had reinforced his understanding of the advertising and sales promotion plans and was able in subsequent discussions with the division manager to convincingly defend his decisions.

Some of Hank's other subordinates were not so lucky. At the risk of reciting the tale of *The Three Little Pigs*, let me relate that those who had fattened their budgets earlier to offset possible action found they suffered unusually large cuts, probably including the $100,000 that Hank had been looking for in Bob's budget. Those who had not built their budgets on a solid foundation of clear-cut objectives lost pieces right and left. And talk about huffing and puffing—one poor soul made a grandstand play by offering *more* in budget reductions than asked for! This manager may have been a hero for a few minutes, but his credibility was suspect in future budget deliberations and the manager later left the company.

CREATE A WIN-WIN ENVIRONMENT

I admit that this early budget review experience (related in the case study) was so etched in my memory that I felt compelled to share it. It underscores the point that bosses can be managed, and managed in a win-win environment. Managing the boss is certainly one of the most personally satisfying experiences in the entire management field and the one with the most immediate and dramatic impact on you and the company's fortunes. You can feel good about helping the boss become a better boss and keeping trouble away from his or her desk.

Regardless of their positive or negative personalities, bosses have some fairly common concerns. Not the least of these is defending and improving the business condition and assuring themselves that their employees are doing likewise. I caught some hint of that in a sign I saw in a San Francisco office:

TO MY STAFF:

I'M CONCERNED ABOUT THE RISING TIDE OF MEDIOCRITY.

YOUR TASK IS TO MAKE SURE THAT IT DOESN'T FLOW INTO THIS OFFICE.

—THE BOSS

MANAGING YOUR STAFF: HIRING AND TRAINING

When you get right down to it, one of the most important tasks of a manager is to eliminate his people's excuse for failure.

—*Robert Townsend*

How is it that some companies seem to attract the brightest and best employees, fill their open job requisitions with good people, then proceed to make them even better than they were when they arrived at the doorstep? It must go beyond the basic principles of hiring and training, but how far beyond? There is evidence that this management task can be mastered simply by gaining a better understanding of "how" to staff, "who" and "what" to look for, and the right questions to ask. With a little guidance, you can become an expert in interviewing, integrating new hires, and turning training tedium into dynamic staff development.

Why do we say managing "staff" rather than managing "employees"? Because staff suggests structure, which can include a business with one or two employees, but also allows for team leaders and middle levels of supervision in a larger organization. By whatever name, it would be difficult, if not foolhardy, to underestimate the importance of this essential business component. As the familiar management saying puts it: "Our most important assets get on the elevator every day at five o'clock and leave the building."

The people who work for you are the vascular system of your business and present a stimulating area of exploration. The area of managing staff is certainly the most inclusive because you have to be involved in the daily activities of the staff. Dealing with staffing issues is where you spend most of the time and includes:

- Selecting employees
- Training and development

- Supervising and motivating
- Evaluating performance

PUTTING PEOPLE IN PERSPECTIVE

If you were to boil down your overall charge as a manager, you would end up with a triangle whose three sides represent planning, action (making decisions), and developing your people.

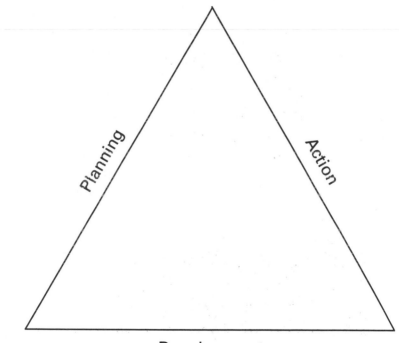

The Management Triangle

Planning

Action

Development

The planning side includes both short-range and long-range plans. It covers visionary thinking that:

- Anticipates problems and formulates steps to deal with them

■ Creates new and improved policies and procedures
■ Conceives of entirely new vectors for the business

Hopefully, you will also have a sense of strategic planning, a realization of the futurity of present actions, and be able to see the future consequence of what is being done today.

The action side is spent largely responding to the demands of the day (i.e., carrying out the plan and reacting to events or to switches thrown by upper-level management) and applying your expertise within your assigned area of responsibility. You will initiate new work, make decisions on projects in the works to advance them toward completion, and apply yourself to controlling budgets and other systems. This activity is more visible than the planning you did behind closed doors and is largely what your boss will use in evaluating your performance.

Finally, you will arrive at the third leg of the triangle—what to do about developing your people. If you are spending all your time planning and doing and scant time in developing your staff, your management job has a hole in it. And if you don't invest the time to coach personnel, they will be doing the job but not learning about it.

FIVE RULES FOR HIRING THE RIGHT PEOPLE

The mechanics of locating qualified people is a snap, and the Internet has made it even easier. With more than 100,000 employment-related sites on the Web posting more than 30 million jobs, help is only a click away. That's not all of it. Computers now conduct many of the initial job interviews. Dozens of big-name retailers such as Target, Macy's, and Home Depot operate computer kiosks that replace paper applications and in-person interviews. The trick, however, is not finding people, but finding the right people from among all those qualified candidates. Let's examine a few of the tried-and-true basics that are timeless.

Rule 1. Hire People Smarter Than You

The obvious alternative is to hire people dumber than you, and who wants to do that? Nevertheless, insecurities come to the surface when a manager starts to consider bright people. When one manager turned down what I thought was an exceptional prospect, I was puzzled and asked why. "I didn't need anybody that good," she replied. Although she could have had a dynamite person at the same price as a lesser prospect, she felt more comfortable bottom fishing. In my judgment, you should hire the best and brightest you can afford and then try to lead them to be even better and brighter.

Failing to hire the best people is self-defeating and, as renowned adman David Ogilvy told his board, "If you always hire people who are smaller than you are, we shall become a company of dwarfs. If, on the other hand, you always hire people who are bigger than you are, we shall become a company of giants."

> Hire the best and brightest, and then try to lead them to become even better and brighter.

Rule 2. Pick Lieutenants That Complement Your Strengths and Compensate Your Weaknesses

Peter Drucker once said, "An effective manager looks at every one of his subordinates and asks, 'What can [they] do?' He doesn't worry too much about what they can't do—he's grateful for every ounce of strength he has in the organization—but above all he looks at himself and asks, 'What is my strength? What do I have to apply? What can I do? How can I staff for my weaknesses?' "

Look first for what's needed to complete your organization. Then look for the best person to fill that position, whether it's someone to complement your strengths or to compensate for your weaknesses. Either way, it's easier to hire winners to begin with, rather than trying to boost mediocre performers to new levels.

Managers also make a hiring error when they look for a complete package. That's when the search is for someone who is well rounded in all aspects, when what they really need is someone who is damn good in accounting. You can use that accounting person to plug a critical weakness in your company even if he or she may never be voted best all-around employee.

Take care, too, that you don't put too much emphasis on style. Sure, you'd like to find people whom you like and who are aligned with your own style. But what the subordinate can do is far more important than personality.

Strangely enough, sometimes your choice of candidates is limited by another curious recruiting hurdle. Believe it or not, on occasion it is difficult to find people who are unlike you. That's because people who are different may not naturally be attracted to you and your style. There may even be the "antagonism of dress," if you're a three-piece suit personality and the would-be applicant is "casual Charlie." You don't start out to pick clones, but your strongest qualities become a magnet for others similarly inclined.

Rule 3. In a Resume, Neatness Counts

You won't learn a whole lot from a resume, but what you do learn may be decisive. One thing I have learned is that it pays to be neat and tidy. My opinion of the applicant takes a huge dip the first time I encounter a typo, gross misspelling (such as the name of the company he says he worked for), or missing word. How will he do a creditable job for my company when he is careless about presenting his most important product—himself? I have a right to expect applicants to be well organized and logical in the resume, as I would expect them to be in the position they seek.

I like to see reference letters but take them with a whole shaker of salt. I have never seen a bad one and I know how people can make themselves sound better than they are. Reference checks should be made, though, to confirm employment and determine if the candidate was truthful in all respects. (Legal constraints limit the amount of other information you will be able to obtain.)

Rule 4. Use the Interview to Get the Facts

In the process, you shouldn't sell too much or tell too much. Early in my career, I made both mistakes. During interviews I was unknowingly guilty of overselling because I was pumped up and passionate about the company and tended to inflate its stature, the importance of the department, and the scope of the specific employment opportunity being discussed.

I made a more grievous error, though, by talking when I should have let the applicant talk. I set myself up by describing the kind of person I was looking for and was amazed to discover that the applicant—like young J. Pierpont Finch in *How to Succeed in Business Without Really Trying*—always seemed to have the precise qualifications I was seeking. The applicants were, obviously, only parroting back what I had told them. I learned quickly to listen after that and to permit the company's personnel professionals to control more of the preliminary screening for me.

The Art of the Interview

The interview is not to be taken lightly and requires preparation on the part of both interviewer and interviewee.

People who interview well typically make very good employees. They have self-confidence and are able to present themselves skillfully. I have noticed that those who interview extremely well have three things in common:

- They always enter with a smile and a firm, friendly handshake that suggests they are truly happy to be there.
- They maintain direct eye contact and remain very focused throughout the interview.
- They respond to questions with brief, upbeat answers and no excuses.

Probe Without Being Predictable

After the applicant's statistical data are recorded (e.g., schooling, present salary), you as the interviewer are ready for the more probing questions. There are literally hundreds of options and you will obviously be searching for plausible answers that relate to the one niche that you have to fill. Phrasing is important. The quality of the question has much to do with the quality of the answer.

> Ask probing questions to elicit detailed information,
> not "yes" or "no" answers.

Managers gain a deeper insight by adding at least a few "situation, action, and result" questions that ask applicants to describe a certain situation they have faced in the past and detail how they have responded to it. For instance, you might ask, "Tell me about a time when you have led a team in a particularly demanding situation, what action the team took, and what the results were." You'll get a great deal more insight than if you merely asked if the applicant has ever led a team in demanding situations.

Above all, as an interviewer you want to avoid asking questions that can be answered yes or no. Ideally the interviewee will provide clear, quantified results and explain how actions and leadership solved a problem and benefited the employer.

Ten Critical Questions for Interviewers

If I had to choose only ten questions, I would go with these:

1. Why do you want this job with this company?
2. How has your education and training prepared you for this position?
3. What are your greatest strengths and weaknesses?
4. How do you think your friends would describe you? Your last supervisor?
5. What is the most difficult situation you have faced in your business career so far and how did you handle it?
6. What has been the biggest disappointment?
7. What is the one trait or skill you possess that should make us pick you over other candidates?
8. What is your idea of success?
9. What do you see yourself doing five or ten years from now?
10. Why are you leaving your present position?

Q-Tip: Sometimes Once Is Not Enough

In the question and answer process, there are certain questions that may need to be asked twice. Take that familiar and inevitable question listed as number ten: Why are you leaving your present position? If the applicant is presently unemployed you will obviously change the tense, but there's something else that should also be changed. It is productive to reach back a little farther in the employment record and also ask why the person left the previous position, and perhaps even the one before that. You can expect to learn three things:

1. *The person's job stability.* You will certainly discover if job changes are happening at fairly frequent intervals.

2. *The reason for the job change.* If each move was markedly different, you may even decipher something from the differences. Suppose the employee is leaving her present employment because she doesn't feel challenged enough, yet exited the previous position because her boss expected too much. An apparent contradiction may be meaningful.

3. *A pattern of similar reasons for job changes.* If there is a problem that seems to be repeating itself, you want to know about it now. If the applicant's last two or three job changes were triggered by differences and dissatisfaction with associates, the problem is typically with the applicant, not the associates.

The important thing is that none of these issues may be evident if you ask only about the one most recent change. At the same time, however, none of the observations are an absolute indication that there is something wrong, so exercise caution and your best judgment. You are taking the applicant's unverified word and, present-day confidentiality policies being what they are, it is unlikely that the specific reasons for termination or departure will be confirmed by a previous employer.

Cover All the Bases

Most interviewers close by also asking, "Do you have any questions for me?" I am always interested in the response and favorably impressed if the applicant has some good questions that demonstrate a willingness to inquire and reflect a serious interest in the job and the company.

Be certain to take notes during the interview, and go over the job description (if you have one) with the applicant to make sure the job scope and responsibilities are clear.

In addition, at least two people should interview each potential candidate to ensure that the best decision is made. A senior manager or experienced personnel person will see things that you don't. Never hesitate to seek counsel from a human resources professional.

Rule 5. It Isn't Over Until It's Over

When the finalist is clearly identified and the offer is made, don't rush to shut the process down too quickly. Make sure you've actually hired the person you want before you turn away the other leading contenders. Just when we thought we had a deal, I've had my top choice decide against the job or accept another one out of the blue. It's much easier to call the second choice and offer that person the job than to have to start the whole process over again. Those clearly out of the running, of course, should be informed as early as possible.

When you feel that the hiring process is complete and your new hire is firmly in place, then you can expeditiously inform the one or two remaining finalists and not leave them hanging. I have always been amazed at the callousness of employers (and there are a lot of them) who forgo the simple courtesy of a letter or phone call to advise rejected applicants whose life may be on hold waiting for a decision.

TRAINING AND DEVELOPING PEOPLE

What kind of fractured logic allocates thousands of dollars to finding people—many of them raw and untested—and then spends pennies on training them? You'll observe it in small businesses, where you might expect it, but it also happens in large corporations where you would least expect it. In the small shop, the owner/manager is close enough to the work and the worker that she can take a personal interest in what is being done. The boss can explain what the employee is expected to do, instruct on methods, and observe the employee's behavior. Best of all, the small business owner/manager can provide immediate feedback on performance. Hopefully, the manager will be able to accomplish all this, acting more as an experienced colleague than as a task master.

Too often, the larger company formalizes the training at the expense of personal hands-on interaction. The manager becomes so busy that the training task is delegated to the company, as in "Wasn't the personnel department going to take care of that?" or "Don't we have in-house training courses anymore?" Be reminded that it is your responsibility as manager to see that your new staff members have the work space, the tools, and the training to perform to the limits of their ability as quickly as possible. As the visionary manager, you are also thinking beyond the employee's ability to become operational this week or this month, and instead are visualizing an exchange in which the employee will contribute energy and independent thinking to benefit the enterprise for years to come.

> Training is *your* responsibility—not "the company's."

Orientation: The First Day of the Rest of Your Business Life

In my judgment, the employee's training and development starts with a warm and positive orientation. You only have one chance to make a good first impression, so make the most of this one. Like a student experiencing the first few days in a new school, the new employee is impressionable and eager to fit in. Your role as manager is to show the employee that he or she is a valuable member of the company, someone who is already respected, and to facilitate the new employee's transition from outsider to insider.

Before that first day on the job, the employee will have received a welcoming letter at home from you that outlines what the first day will be like and who will be doing what. It can serve as a checklist as the employee proceeds through the day and help to address key questions. Depending on the size of the company, there may be more human resources department involvement or a formal orientation procedure as well. Regardless, you should make it a point to become as personally and actively involved as possible.

On the first day, you should have cleared your calendar to permit, at the very least, your personal introduction of the new employee. Do not delegate this responsibility to someone else. Advise others when the new employee will start and take the responsibility for introducing the new person to coworkers and to the highest-level executive you feel is appropriate and accessible. (Even if the big boss is surprised by your gesture, she will be impressed by the extent to which you are an involved "people person.") The opportunity to interact with someone from upper management gives the newcomer instant acceptance and can buy an enormous amount of loyalty. Imagine the pride the employee has in saying, "I met the CEO today and we had a nice chat."

Follow your orientation plan, but don't overwhelm the new employee on the first day. Empathize with the confusion over new names, titles, places, policies, and terminology. (We started providing a list of company acronyms after a new hire confided, "I'll be all right as soon as I find out what language they're speaking around here." The employee was justified in his concern. How would you react if a coworker were to say,

"If the DSG product is on Answer-Pak, you'd better check with AISSD.") Encourage the new hire to ask questions. Be patient and show respect by being a good listener. And always wrap up the first day with a relaxed review of where the process is and what is planned for day two.

Don't let the orientation become a one-day event and then just fade away. Continue to monitor and guide the orientation, with frequent checkpoints, over the days or weeks it takes to unfold. Sit down with the employee after a week, for instance, and ask how the first week has gone and what you and the other staff can do to make the time more productive. Encourage the person to keep a list of questions to be answered and to have an unhurried question and answer session with you at a convenient time.

Training and Empowerment

The subject of training employees in the twenty-first century is too broad a canvas to cover succinctly in one chapter or even one book. But we can find one patch of common ground, and that lies in the manager's dedication to empowering the employee. Sure, all managers would like to get the person trained in a hurry, up to speed and fully functioning within the operating business unit. Managers would also like for the new hire to feel at home and settle into a long-term employment track. That's the way managers used to do it, and the new employee dutifully accepted whatever training was thrown his or her way. But today's manager realizes that this is not the employee or workplace of yesteryear.

Employer-Employee Partnership

Today's emphasis is on increased independent actions and decision making by the employee. Training and development, by whatever name it is called, must result in an employee who has a feeling of ownership in his or her work and who will apply personal creativity and thinking to ensure continuous improvement in the work process. It entails more give-and-take, more listening; it means shaping a new employer-employee partnership. In too many cases, the toughest obstacle doesn't come from the employee but from the manager, because the manager struggles with a new management paradigm built on influencing and leading rather than controlling and directing.

> The new model of training emphasizes coaching and empowering employees to make decisions and take risks.

There will be specialized technical training commensurate with the work responsibilities, but in the new workforce the bulk of the training will more likely be delivered as coaching. In the traditional model, the manager was the unquestioned authority and source of all knowledge. The manager trained and led by directive and employees listened and did as they were told. Coaching recognizes first of all that the boss doesn't know the answer to every problem. No one does. Business is too complex and continuous improvement requires the continuous exchange of information among all contributors—vertically and horizontally, across all levels and between all disciplines. The assembly worker, the inspector, and the worker on the shipping dock all have ideas that can improve the product and raise customer satisfaction. Small wonder that input from the field sales representative, who is closest to the customer, now gets fed back and is actually considered by engineers in product development. The summum bonum, or supreme good, for all employees becomes serving the customer rather than making sales or squeezing another dollar of profit. If we serve the customer well, those other goals will be duly realized in the process. In this environment, training is based on encouraging employees to make decisions and to take intelligent risks.

Make Training a Mixed Bag

Many managers still prefer to leave training to the trainers, and in a larger organization the manager may be able to do that. Ideally, your employee training and development program will include the manager's personal participation, training generated in-house by other contributors, pertinent instruction from outside experts, continuing voluntary involvement by the trainee in professional organizations, on-the-job mentoring from an experienced peer-partner, and frequent and open exchange of ideas in team sessions.

A well-balanced mix of all available training and development resources, within a well-constructed and measurable program, will result in a learning experience that is both effective and enjoyable for manager as well as new employee.

CHAPTER

6

MANAGING YOUR STAFF: LEADING, MOTIVATING, EVALUATING, AND REWARDING

Don't tell people how to do things. Tell them what to do and
let them surprise you with their results.

—*George S. Patton*

Have you ever attended a motivational seminar that lifted you to a fever pitch, then suffered leakage before you reached the parking lot? Retaining the buzz is difficult enough, and transferring it top-down to your staff is next to impossible. The key is a bottom-up management approach that satisfies ten worker needs and permits workers to motivate themselves. As part of the deal, the manager winds up with a redefined leadership role and a team of people who, would you believe it, actually admit that they love their jobs.

Customary wisdom says that the manager's job deals with effectiveness whereas the supervisor's job deals with efficiency. The manager is the ivory-tower visionary deciding what things need to be done while the supervisor deals directly with employees to get those things done—to meet production quotas and schedules, for instance. We all know that the distinctions are nowhere that clear-cut and that the manager spends time—a lot of it—in face-to-face interaction with employees at all levels. We know that the manager is a hybrid part-time executive, part-time supervisor, and part-time doer, striving all the while to maintain a perspective as the organization's leader.

The really tough part is that the manager has to get down into the trenches with employees, but also has to maintain communication links and relationships upward to bosses and laterally to counterparts in other company departments and functions. The latter area is sometimes called boundary management because it deals not only with managing the recognized borders with other departments, but also traversing the invisible borders or demarcation lines around one functional group or another within the organization (an example is those who may, regardless of their departmental affiliation, call themselves "computer people"). The manager needs the cooperation and support of all groups, formal or informal.

Let's detach the manager (temporarily) from those upward and lateral considerations and concentrate only on the intramural duties within the walls of the manager's own department. To get a feel for the issues in this localized constituency, we'll forget for the moment about strategic thinking and just stick to the daily handling of the organization and its members. But be prepared for a surprise: What we learn about how the manager works in these situations can serve as a strong indicator in two unexpected areas.

THE "L" WORD

In launching this book, I promised myself that there were two subjects that I would not tackle head-on. The first was leadership. The reason was simple: Answering the question, "What makes a leader?" is incredibly difficult. This book is a treatise on management, but not an encyclopedia of management. Pontificating about leadership qualities would renege on my promise in the introduction that I would not give you more tools than you can carry.

It's not that I haven't brooded about leadership and its intrinsic traits, such as command presence, a see-around-the-corner ability to anticipate events, unflappability under fire (from corporate fusillades as well as bullets), and charisma. (There's even one skill that is seldom mentioned—the leader's ability to achieve consensus, something usually drawn from a sensitivity to all sides of an issue and a 360-degree awareness of how all players feel about a situation.) About as quickly as you can identify one attribute as being a necessary leadership component, a hundred examples come along to knock it down. The more you look at historical models, the less they seem to fit reality. For every courtly, inspiring Robert E. Lee, there is a slouching, stubborn Ulysses S. Grant. Go figure. Even the U.S. Marines, who once idolized John Wayne's over-the-top "Who wants to live forever" bravado as the model for leadership in combat, have given way to a more cerebral model of a leader as one who commands and controls his troops, and not necessarily by dashing out in front of them.

THE "M" WORD

The other subject I dubbed off-limits was motivation, a topic no less expansive and equally elusive. There are assertive, supremely confident motivators and there are quiet, seemingly detached motivators. Some people respond reasonably well to fear as a motivator while others say it takes caring, not scaring, and opt for nurturing and support. Some are moved by reward and others by recognition. Perhaps the writer was correct who said, "I'm not sure you can really motivate people long term. Maybe the best you can do is create an environment in which they can motivate themselves."

WHAT DO THOSE PEOPLE WANT?

Having made those exclusions and vowing not to try to define leadership and motivation, I was quite surprised by my own epiphany, an experience that began when I recalled once overhearing an exasperated art and production manager complain about his staff. "What do those people want?" he anguished. As I chased that question in this chapter, recollecting the things I had learned about what staff found important, I got a glimpse of a separate reality. It dawned on me that managers who most successfully meet the everyday needs of their staff are the ones who are most often considered good leaders and motivators. Although I am not backtracking and attempting a detailed analysis of those two subjects, I am suggesting that the sum total of the following ten things that managers seek to consistently provide to their staff also provides a curious equation:

$$S = M + L$$

or

Supplying Employee Needs = Motivation + Leadership

> Meeting your employees' everyday needs —
> motivation and leadership.

Ten Things Employees Want

Respect

Respect is made up of many things, not the least of which are the trust managers place in employees, the amount of empowerment and freedom employees have, and the reward received. There are more subtle signs of respect, beginning with a title. I refer to "employees" throughout this book as a generic term and a literary expediency. In the real world, though, employers may choose to use more respectful titles. At Disney, employees are "cast members." At Wal-Mart, they are "associates." In a religious order, they are "brothers" and "sisters." You show respect if you apply a meaningful title for members of your workforce.

Another simple starting place for the manager to show respect is to know everyone's name and to say "good morning" every day. In other words, treat staff members as trusted associates rather than distant subordinates.

Listening to their suggestions, and their complaints, is an obvious mark of respect. You must acknowledge employee suggestions, even if you don't agree with them.

Providing employees with good working conditions and equipment, giving them training to improve their skills, keeping them informed of company business strategies, involving them in the decision-making process, and giving recognition for performance are all evidence that you respect individual employees and value their contribution.

Ownership of Environment

Employees want to feel they have a home, not just a temporary place in line. Even if it's just the ten-foot by ten-foot cubicle that Dilbert immortalized, put the person's name on it. Let employees decorate their own office or work space. If they want to dress up the lunchroom or add some creature comfort, show them you're willing to spend some money to meet their needs. (I visited a corporation in Connecticut where upper-executive offices were tastefully decorated and furnished to the executive's personal tastes. One would question how a company can justify that opulence and expect lower-tier employees to work in a barracks environment.) Let employees have a work space in which they can take pride. This applies to temporary staff, too. It enhances their productivity and your reputation.

Let employees know they have control over their environment. When our company consolidated several departments to create a single source for art and printing services, we let the employees determine the layout, interior design, name, and logo for the new entity: the corporate graphics center. They worked hard for this business site because they owned it. Ownership fuels a feeling of empowerment that says to the employee, "You have control over your space and your job. You can make decisions about your work that make you more effective. You have the ability and the freedom to improve the process and materially contribute to the company's progress."

A Sense of Affiliation

People want to be part of something, to be affiliated with others in a team or clan. You can encourage that identification by letting them "name" themselves. This is especially helpful in breaking down walls within a cross-functional team composed of members from different parts of the company. That's how a team of folks working on difficult IT (information technology) problems came to call themselves "The Nutcrackers" and prided themselves in their identity. The military is rife with names that are applied to individual units, and college football teams would be colorless without a Crimson Tide or Golden Hurricane. Even in small units within a company, a unique identity can provide a stronger sense of belonging.

There are many other ways to fashion a feeling of kinship and to bring everyone into the group. Let people dress down on Fridays or whenever they feel like it. Create T-shirts that identify your company or your team within the company. Have company outings and picnics on a regular basis. Observe birthdays and any other kind of special day, such as an employee's anniversary with the company. Set up friendly competition with other departments or contests within your own area. Employees want to feel like they are part of a family and—borrowing from *Cheers*—they want to go "where everybody knows your name."

Fair Compensation

Is it just me, or doesn't it sometimes seem that the pendulum has swung too far away from the issue of pay? "What does the job pay?" used to be a prime consideration. Some human resources people are quick to point out that what employees really want is recognition, involvement, and appreciation from the employer. They say that in a study of the ten most important concerns for employees, money is rated in about the middle.

Be that as it may, I'm convinced you won't attract or retain good employees for long unless they feel they are being fairly compensated for their time. Reduced to basics, the whole pay issue is a process of exchange, in which the person exchanges labor for money. If the employee values the effort being expended, then there is a clear expectation of a commensurate level of reward.

Psychic Rewards

The employee must also receive nontangible rewards for achievement, most notably recognition, and it should be proffered both publicly in-person and in other company communications. We all know to praise in public and criticize in private and to follow the advice of *The One Minute Manager* and catch people doing something right and dispense immediate praise. There are additional ways you can recognize contributors, though. They include:

- Posting a list of accomplishments in the department
- Presenting awards
- Paying for an unexpected training course for a deserving employee
- Sending an employee to a convention
- Paying for membership dues in a professional society
- Giving employees your reserved parking space for a week
- Awarding compensatory time off for projects that entailed long hours

If not more important than pay, psychic rewards certainly rank right up there.

Straight Talk

The employee is entitled to expect clear, unambiguous guidance and communication from the boss. That goes for bad news as well as good news. (Some managers are great about passing out good news but disappear when it comes to bad news.) In either instance, you must communicate directly and quickly, or face the consequences—letting the grapevine take over!

If you ignore the grapevine it can become the primary source of company information. The manager cannot abolish it entirely, but you can control it by maintaining good personal communications with your employees and keeping employees fully informed about company decisions and policies. (This means, of course, that first you have to keep yourself fully informed on what's happening.) Listening relates to more than just grasping company news. It also includes making sure that the employee clearly understands personal work objectives and other elements of the position. Remember, too, that research proves conclusively that when communication improves so does motivation.

Stay in touch, control rumors, and establish a reputation for truthfulness. Get the grapevine on your side by being a ready, reliable source of information whenever you're approached, in the shop or in the parking lot.

Realize that many employees like to complain about the boss, and even your best intentions won't stop all of it. Your straight talk, though, will head off problems and dry up the grapevine instead of nurturing it.

Visibility at the Top

The trouble with many organizations is that the captain is up on the bridge while the employees are down below the waterline. When the commander is out of sight and out of touch, the crew becomes restless. You can remedy that situation by engaging in management by walking around and more eyeball-to-eyeball contact. You need to walk the plant or offices to instill confidence and to find out what's going on. The benefits are enormous—you'll get the good news first, which is nice, but you'll also get the bad news first, and that's pivotal. You'll pick up scuttlebutt and informal communications that would never pass through the filter of written messages and memos. If you choose to dialogue, you'll also be accessible to answer questions and provide the kind of straight talk employees value highly.

Empathy

Someone has said that employees don't care how much you know until they know how much you care. Sympathy is feeling sorry about their pain. Empathy is feeling their pain. Anytime you can actually put yourself in the other person's shoes, you have reached a defining moment in the relationship. I have known a few managers like that—who knew what was important to their employees and were sensitive to their emotional needs. These are the managers who aren't embarrassed to celebrate your small successes, remember birthdays and anniversaries, send a personal note on special occasions, or attend a funeral instead of just sending a card. One of my first bosses went out of his way to be caring in such a situation, and it bought an incredible amount of personal loyalty. Never underestimate the value of empathy.

Trust and Safety

Employees want to feel that they have a reasonable degree of security and are not about to lose their job at any minute. While some managers fret over workers sinking into a comfort zone, you can't expect to elicit aggressive performance from someone who fears punishment for the first mistake. In the final analysis, mistakes—and the way they are handled—may be the best barometer of trust in the employee.

As Dr. Arnold Beckman has said, "If an employee isn't making any mistakes, he must not be doing much."

Of course, the question is often, "How big a mistake is allowable?" Some workers can get in trouble over a $100 mistake while others can walk away unscathed from a $10,000 slip. As you might imagine, the difference is in the individual's perceived value to the organization, the inherent risk/reward in the situation, the value of what was learned from the mistake, and management's response to the situation. Each mistake is a learning experience, but it is also an opportunity for the manager to show how much trust and confidence is vested in the employee.

In my own experience, I have gambled on employees whose mistakes warranted termination, such as a middle manager who, while under the influence, crashed a company car into the side of a tavern. After a reprimand and soul-searching discussion, I opted to keep the employee and went to bat for him with the company. He had a problem that he addressed successfully and bounced back to become one of the most effective executives in the corporation. He concluded a model career with more than twenty years of valuable and clean-and-sober service, and I am quite sure that an act of trust provided much of the momentum in this turnaround. Your employees will go that extra mile for you if you demonstrate your faith in them.

Favoritism . . . for Everyone

Show favoritism for everyone? How is that possible? Listen to the words of Los Angeles Lakers coach Phil Jackson, who has created two professional basketball dynasties:

> Everybody is treated differently the same. How does that make sense? You have to have the same set of rules, but everybody gets treated differently because they are different people. And, as a consequence, you

try to adapt what you are trying to do so that everybody will fit in a way that makes them feel personalized.*

The veteran coach takes players with disparate personalities,
some of them "problem children," and inspires them by treating them equally—but appealing to the highest aspirations
within each individual. He makes them feel as if they are his
favorites. Players say that they know Jackson has their best
interests in mind, not just another championship.

As a manager, you must tailor your coaching to each
employee's individual needs, but still treat everyone the same.
Guard against singling out favorites by making them all your
favorites. That's how you'll build your championship team.

THE LEADER/MOTIVATOR PORTRAIT

There you have it—ten needs fulfilled for employees. But
don't forget the surprise in the package! What you also have
is a partially completed portrait of a leader and motivator.
Like a paint-by-the-numbers picture, you have ten numbers
colored in. The remaining numbers are the givens and a few
electives—technical competence, forward thinking, intelli-
gence, force and assertiveness, and command presence—plus
several unknowns that relate specifically to that job. The
leader in a banking environment will likely have some specific
qualities quite different from those of a pro football coach.
The motivational manager who can drive a tough construc-
tion crew may not look anything like the inspirational research director who can energize a group of scientists.

Nevertheless, if you have met the ten needs of the employees and painted in at least a few of the remaining areas,

*Kevin Ding. "Phil Jackson." *Orange County Register*, 5 December 2000, pp. 5–9.

you will have an image of leadership and motivation that looks a lot like . . . *you.*

EVALUATING AND REWARDING PERFORMANCE

Matching performance to pay has come a long way in the past century. In olden days, worker evaluation was rudimentary. If you were performing up to expectations, you kept your job and occasionally got a bonus or small pay hike. If you weren't performing, you might be gone. People tended to work incredibly hard and stay with one company for their entire working career, with their children often serving as apprentices and following them into the occupation. Personnel records left much to be desired and, like the debtor to the company store, you may have remained fettered to the job because you were always in debt to it.

> Follow four basic steps for evaluating and rewarding performance.

Not so today. A new day has dawned in enlightened human resources management with inclusive employment laws and regulations, clear job classifications, salary surveys, tiers of incentives and bonuses, and a myriad of revolutionary evaluation and compensation programs. As a manager, it is helpful if you are conversant with the new realities or at least have a creditable human resources person or outside resource to turn to. Here I address only the survival-level basics that I've found useful in evaluating an employee's performance and providing compensation within a merit system. They include four steps.

1. Proof of performance
2. Appraisal
3. Determination of compensation
4. The review meeting

These steps resemble a recipe that reads "Take two eggs . . ." and proceeds to list the rest of the ingredients. So get out your bowls and get ready to begin a typical employee evaluation.

Proof of Performance

1. *Take one job classification.* The classification should be shaped by analysis to determine at what pay level the job is positioned within the company's overall framework of salaried and hourly positions. This is the financial foundation of the compensation process.

2. *Take one fully developed job description.* It should clearly describe the employee's duties and responsibilities.

3. *Take five or six specific work objectives that were set for the time period covered.* These measurable objectives are usually extracted from the major areas of responsibility identified in the job description. Ideally, these objectives will be balanced so that none are overemphasized and each is weighted to indicate what percentage of the total it represents.

4. *Add in a written accomplishment report from the employee.* This is the employee's statement as to how well he or she has met each objective during the review period. The employee should supply clear, quantitative proof of success.

Now the manager has the reference data required for the next step: the evaluation of the employee's performance vis-à-vis the stated objectives.

Appraisal

This is the stage of the process in which the manager adds in her own experience and observation of the employee's work. The manager has the employee's statement of accomplishment in hand, but must determine just how realistic that is. Avoid relying on impressions rather than facts. Avoid holding the employee responsible for events beyond his or her control. If the manager is not completely familiar with the results, she will investigate further. When she has a clear picture of the accomplishments, she can rate each as to whether they were unsatisfactory, below average, satisfactory, good, above average, or outstanding. A satisfactory accomplishment, for example, only says that the employee did what would ordinarily be expected of a person in that position. In a typical organization, six or seven out of ten employees will fall into a satisfactory or average range. Tip: If average sounds demeaning, say "fully meets job requirements."

As the manager, you will compare the employee's performance on your scale ranging from unsatisfactory to outstanding. The more experienced managers sometimes apply another measure—comparing the employee's performance against a phantom employee, which is the very best person they have ever observed in that particular position. This historical recollection may become your new standard for outstanding. Although not as quantifiable, this technique can bring a dose of reality into a tie-breaker decision.

For most appraisals, just clustering people in a handful of classifications (like "average" or "satisfactory") is not good enough. Distinguishing between workers in this group doesn't tell us whether they are the best of the worst or the worst of the best. Or something quite different altogether. There is a need for scoring and ranking if the process is to be meaningful.

The answer? Bring in the metrics. If, as a new manager,

you're evaluating only one or two employees, you'll have a relatively clear measure of their performance. If, however, you have several people similarly positioned, you will need a device to value each quantitatively. Performance appraisal forms are intended to help you do that, and offer several variations on a theme. Some list various critical factors that relate to the employee's job description, such as productivity, accuracy, initiative, and attitude and, relying on the employee's report or on memory, the manager rates the employee on each count.

The rating system that I prefer is built upon specific work objectives, as few as two and no more than ten, that were developed way back at the beginning of the review period. The objectives are derived from the key elements of the employee's position description. If, for instance, the position description flags accuracy as a critical responsibility of the employee's job, then one work objective for this time period will be to achieve a certain error rate. Since all objectives are weighted to indicate their relative degree of importance to the overall requirements of the position, and accuracy is more important in this instance than any other responsibility, the assigned error rate objective will carry the highest weighting.

A typical example in the chart below shows an appraisal of six specific objectives, each rated by the manager on a scale to 100 (see point scale), and each weighted according to importance. A point total is the end result.

OBJECTIVE	SCORE	WEIGHT	TOTAL
#1	75	10%	7.5
#2	60	20%	12.0
#3	85	15%	12.75
#4	60	35%	21.0
#5	90	5%	4.5
#6	65	15%	9.75
		100%	67.5

POINT SCALE FOR SCORE
Outstanding (far exceeds expectations) .... 90 to 100
Above Average (meets or exceeds
    expectations) .... 70 to 90
Average (satisfactorily meets normal
    requirements) .... 50 to 70
Below Average (inadequate, needs to
    improve) .... 40 to 50
Unsatisfactory (requires serious remedial
    action) .... below 40

This result is no longer "just in the neighborhood" but is fixed at a specific number, a point total of 67.5. Some other dynamics are also in evidence. In this example, the employee's modest performance did not capitalize on the opportunity presented by objective #4, the task of greatest impact and weight. When the employee did perform to an outstanding level (objective #5), it happened to be one of lesser importance that was weighted accordingly. Bear in mind that these objectives, as well as their weights, have been visible to the employee throughout the entire year or whatever review period is being evaluated.

Yes, specific numbers are important to accurately appraise performance and to determine compensation, particularly when there are similar employees who share in the compensation pool.

Compensation: Splitting the Pot

Plans for awarding pay increases vary widely, aside from those that may be mandated contractually, union influenced, or supplemented by bonuses and other special awards. The timing also varies. Some companies go through the review process on the anniversary of the employee's hiring. More large companies prefer to evaluate all employees on a given schedule or to review all salaried employees at one time of the year and hourly personnel on their employment anniversaries. Although conducting performance reviews at one time of the year places a large burden on the manager and on the human resources department, its advantages offset the inconvenience. It forces the event to be a top priority and enables the manager to more easily compare people side by side and to realistically evaluate their contribution.

In a large company, the total amount of money available for pay increases is something that is decided by top management and the chief human resources executive, sometimes in a compensation committee composed of top management and others, perhaps even with the oversight of a member of the board. The result is that the merit pay pool (assuming your company uses a merit pay system) for that year consists of a certain percentage of the total payroll. For example, the magic number for that review may be 4.5 percent. That says that 4.5 percent of the existing annual payroll for those hundreds or thousands of employees being reviewed has been set aside in a pool to be distributed among them in merit pay increases. Since it is a merit system and not an across-the-board flat increase to everyone, it also says that some will receive more than others and some may receive nothing. With a 4.5 percent merit pool, it stands to reason that for each diligent worker who earns a 6 percent or more increase, another lower-rated employee will see 3 percent or less.

Within the compensation mechanics of most large companies, there are exceptions. If you have an unusually capable employee whose work far, far exceeds others, you can apply to personnel for a special increase outside the bounds of the normal policy. Yet another exception: If the person is really good, perhaps he or she should be promoted to a higher-level classification. The advantage in doing so is that the salary action becomes part of a promotional increase and is ordinarily not taken from the normal pool—thus leaving the pool for you to use with other people.

One thing you must never do is to let bias and outside factors influence the administration of the pay process. Be cautious about overweighting something like the person working long hours. Hopefully, it is a sign of zealous dedication to the job. But that isn't always the case. Is it because the employee isn't getting a day's work done within the normal workday? Is it the case of an unhappy person escaping into her work? (One study at least suggests that unhappy marriages frequently result in spouses working longer hours since work is a more comfortable place than home in those situations.)

Do not be swayed by factors that have nothing to do with performance: race, gender, age, or the employee's personal circumstances. The rule here is "each according to performance, not each according to need." You may feel quite certain that the struggling single parent needs the raise more than another employee who appears very comfortable financially, but that is not your decision to make. You can address the welfare of your staff in other ways, but the compensation review is not the time.

Conducting the Review Meeting

One of the manager's personal aims should be to make the performance review discussion a positive and productive meeting. It is, without doubt, the one time in the year when you will have the employee's undivided attention. You would like to make it an encounter that is not intimidating but will even be greatly anticipated by the participants, yourself included. A good performance appraisal will leave both parties feeling that they have gained something. For that to happen, the following conditions must exist:

■ The review must be the culmination of an orderly, unhurried process in which the employee and the reviewer have had ample time to prepare.

- The manager must use the experience not only to recognize present accomplishment, but to point the way to future improvement.

- The review must focus on the employee's performance, not how the employee feels about others in the company or how the manager feels about the employee personally.

- The employee must feel that he or she is participating in the review and that an open, two-way dialogue exists.

- The reviewer must be candid and support conclusions with facts.

> A good performance review meeting leaves both parties feeling they have gained something.

Where to Begin the Discussion

Begin, of course, with a greeting and an effort to relax tensions. Create a comfortable atmosphere. Provide some favorable, disarming comment on how much you value this member of your staff.

Provide a brief and simple overview of the performance review and compensation process in general, encouraging questions and interaction on any areas that might be unclear. Take things in order—do not jump to the ratings or the pay action before the performance has been fully discussed.

Before starting your appraisal of the person's accomplishment, remind the employee that the objectives set for the year were codeveloped with the employee. There should be no surprises about what was expected, and it is a little late for any employee to challenge an objective during the review meeting. Then go through the objectives one by one, stating your assessment of each and referring often to the employee's own words as supplied in the report. If you are not getting feedback from the employee, ask frequently for opinions. You must ask employees to explain how well they met that assignment or how they think they might have done it better. Ask also what you could have done to make the job easier.

Be frank about credibility gaps. Suppose, for example, that supervisor Frank had accepted a work objective to plan, budget, and transform a vacant storeroom into a departmental training room. As noted in his accomplishment report, the desired training room was implemented and is being used productively as you had expected. Now here's the rub: You happen to know that Frank procrastinated, handled the project poorly, and was late getting others involved in the project. His assistant had to salvage the project and, almost in spite of Frank, carried it through to completion. Obviously, you will clearly point out the discrepancy. Frank gets no brownie points for that one.

In each instance, try to focus on the employee's strengths first and then provide feedback on areas of weakness and how they might be corrected. Don't pound on the person's weakness as a personal deficiency but relate it to the department's performance and how it affects others. I had an art department manager who tended to be surly and abrupt with in-house customers, which affected his job reviews negatively. He had great difficulty accepting that his style was a problem until it was shown that the art department was losing business to outside suppliers who treated these customers with more civility and respect. Understanding that the team was jeopardized by his actions isolated the problem and awakened a new sensitivity to improved customer service. There is no progress until the person first acknowledges that a problem truly exists.

Show Me the Money

When the discussion gets around to money—and it always does—you will follow the same measured procedure as in the previous discussion about performance issues. This is, after all, just an extension of the earlier discussion and quantifies the performance in terms of pay. The focus shifts smoothly to reward and, if the preceding communication has been clear, there should also be no big surprises over pay. If you give an above-average review, then you should give an above-average raise. The thing you will want to avoid is laying too many positive comments on a weak or marginal employee, thereby giving the impression that a raise is merited. If we say only nice things about an employee and then give a low raise, we appear to be inconsistent.

Always have the employee sign the completed evaluation. It confirms that the employee has received it, even if he or she may not agree with it.

HOW MUCH VALUE CAN YOU ADD?

In this important management ritual of evaluating and compensating employees, you must ask yourself, "Have I been totally fair and unbiased? Have I treated the employee with dignity? Have I treated the employee in a way that, in the long run, will benefit both the individual and the company?" While others may consider employees as merely being disposable or recyclable and treat the evaluation process as a mere formality, you see it differently. You hold yourself to a higher standard and should always think of your staff as being "enhanceable." That is, there will be value added and you will achieve value from these individuals beyond what they represented when they joined your team. The way you handle sensitive personnel issues is influential in moving your people toward that goal. It's one of the keys to a business organization that grows and thrives and continually improves itself.

7

MANAGING
MEETINGS

The farmer has his field; the worker has his machines;
the businessman has his meetings.

—*How to Succeed in Business Without Really Trying*

Managers have a love-hate relationship with meetings. They apparently love them enough to spend hours closeted in these sessions, immediately after which they bemoan the lost time. Too bad, because—as you will see—only a few minutes of study can establish guidelines that boost meeting productivity by leaps and bounds. It isn't all that difficult to identify which meetings are essential, who should attend, and how they should be conducted in order to save you time and money.

When was the first meeting in history? Using the biblical example, it was in the Garden of Eden after God had completed his creation. (Some meetings are called right after the work is done, instead of before it. Of necessity, this one had to follow the creation or God wouldn't have had anyone to talk to.)

After completing the universe, God made man and woman in his image and met with them. He did it the right way, too. He used the first meeting as an opportunity to uplift and inform. He first "blessed them" and then presented some clear goals and objectives: "Be fruitful, and multiply, and replenish the earth, and subdue it." Then God proceeded to spell out the opportunities abounding in the new world, plus a couple of restrictions. The meeting went well and God and the participants were pleased.

The second meeting didn't go so well. By then Adam and Eve had disobeyed God and tried to pass up this meeting. What followed instead was passing alright, but it was something called passing the buck, a practice that persists to this day whenever people mess up. When God asked Adam who goofed, Adam blamed it on "the woman whom thou gavest to be with me." When the woman was asked, she said, "The serpent beguiled me." God obviously saw through the whole thing and evicted them from the Garden. One moral of the story is this: Some meetings are better than others. In this chapter, I share some thoughts that may help you have more good meetings and almost no bad ones.

WHEN IS A MEETING A MEETING?

In identifying the territory, let's begin by eliminating the parts that are outside the borders of our exploration. What constitutes a business meeting and what contact is either too casual to be considered here or too large to get into the tent? When is a meeting a meeting? I suspect it happens whenever:

- The encounter is a planned and scheduled occurrence.
- There is a specific issue at hand.
- The people who can make or influence a decision are in attendance.

That arbitrarily excludes the impromptu contact between two people in the hall, not because that meeting can't produce results (it often does) but because there's little you or I can do to improve the process. As a manager, you can't prepare for it and there are few ground rules to add any real semblance of order to it.

We also exclude the large meeting (more than twenty people) for a different reason. When a gathering reaches a certain size, it becomes an event—an assembly, seminar, sales meeting, or conference—but it is not a business meeting over which you exert the same level of control. Free and open discussion among participants is also likely to be limited. Certainly there are exceptions, and some people will argue that videoconferencing may include many participants and still ac-commodate close interaction. I'm sure it happens, but in my experience the technology gets in the way, whether we like it or not.

The meetings that offer the most fertile area for study are the basic, generic type—typically with four to twenty partici-pants—that you call, schedule, and chair. After all, we are looking at hands-on management issues and those meetings are the ones you best manage and control.

WHY ARE MEETINGS CALLED TIME WASTERS?

What is it with these meetings, anyway? I was notified one afternoon by a senior manager about a meeting he had called for the following morning. As he was leaving my office, he commented almost apologetically, "We could probably get a lot done if it weren't for all these meetings." Since he was the one calling most of the meetings, this self-incrimination seemed odd to me. Unfortunately, it is commonplace.

> **Meetings are a necessary evil that we haven't learned to control and can't do without.**

Universally, managers single out meetings as the biggest time waster on the job, yet midlevel managers say they spend 25 percent to 30 percent of their workday in meetings of one kind or another. Why do we devote so much time and energy to something that we claim is so wasteful? The answer must be that the meeting is a necessary evil that we haven't learned to control and can't do without. As the true cost of meetings is being scrutinized more closely, increased attention is being given to alternatives to on-site meetings—options that do not require staff to travel to a central location or be away from work for extended periods of time. These alternatives may include videoconferencing, conference calls, and chat rooms. Yet don't expect them to do away with face-to-face meetings. The fact remains: Meetings are essential for communication and decision making and most managers realize it. Otherwise, they wouldn't get so irate when they're left out of one.

IS THIS MEETING NECESSARY?—STEPS TO ENSURE A PRODUCTIVE MEETING

The first step in meeting planning is to ask if we even need a meeting. What is the objective, and is a meeting the best way to reach it? What are the alternatives? Would a phone call serve as well? Have we considered the total cost in preparation time and travel time, as well as meeting time? Once you have determined that a meeting is the best solution and the best use of the participants' time, then you can go about the following steps to ensure that the meeting delivers maximum productivity.

What Is the Objective?

You must have a stated purpose for the meeting. If it is a formal, scheduled meeting, then that objective should be defined in a prepared agenda. Agenda items should be clearly stated and specific enough for attendees to understand (e.g., don't say "work hours" will be discussed if you mean to discuss "flextime for hourly employees"). The agenda, usually accompanied by a meeting announcement memo, should be distributed far enough in advance so that the participants can prepare for it. The memo and agenda should include the objective, the place of the meeting, the time it will begin and end, the participants, and what preparation is expected.

In a more extended meeting, such as a daylong management meeting, I have even stated objectives for individual parts of the meeting and made them a part of the prepared agenda. The agenda should indicate (from left to right across the page):

■ The time period for that topic
■ The topic (often with a subhead to add more clarity)
■ The presenter or discussion leader
■ The objective (i.e., what we expect to accomplish) for that specific discussion (usually written in the far right column)

Who Should Attend?

Limit the invitations to the minimum number of people needed to accomplish the objective. That will vary somewhat, depending on whether the nature of the meeting is informational, planning, problem solving, or policy making. The most critical, for instance, is the meeting to make decisions on policy—decisions that may have far-reaching consequences. In this case, if you are attempting to sell an idea or reach a favorable decision, then you want to create a balance and include participants favorable to your interests. You need to know who favors your proposal and who will oppose it, and you are obligated to invite some of the latter in order to ensure a fair discussion. If a crucial vote or outcome is expected from the meeting, you may also wish to add weight by including a technical expert or higher-level executive favorable to your position, provided that the inclusion does not appear inappropriate and raise the question, "Why is this person here?"

How Many Should Be Invited?

Again, include only those who need to be there. Four to seven is an ideal number for most planning meetings. An informational briefing or a training session can have many more attendees. In a planning meeting where discussion is anticipated and welcomed, the more people you invite, the longer the meeting becomes. Although meeting length was not the primary reason for excluding larger group meetings of twenty or more people from this chapter, it is also true that the more participants, the more difficult it is to achieve your objective. Small groups permit more candor and sharing. Larger groups lead to more "performing" by members and the real meaning becomes lost in the theatrics.

What's the Best Seating Arrangement?

For most meetings this is not a major concern, but it always exerts some influence on the proceedings. Ideally, participants would be seated in a circle to encourage participation. Since this is not always practical or possible, any reasonable arrangement is acceptable that facilitates good eye contact and recognizes the human dynamics in the situation. No one should feel out of the loop. The spatial relationship between the discussion leader and the participants should not have a pulpit-congregation feel to it. The screen, television, or audiovisual equipment should be functional but not dominate the room.

In policy-making meetings, seating arrangement may take on a more strategic role. You can set up the room to prevent power brokering, control troublemakers, or merely suppress annoying whispering or disturbance. For a formal meeting, I would normally make up a personalized meeting folder or binder that would be placed at each attendee's table place. With the person's name clearly visible on the front of the folder, there is no question that this folder and this seat are intended for a specific individual. With proper arrangement and positioning of the participants, the champions can contain the malcontents and the meeting is freed from those who would shoot down every idea. This is not a radical new idea—schoolteachers discovered long ago that two troublemakers seated together feed on each other and can destroy a class. I just don't want it to happen in my classroom.

THE DYNAMICS OF SMALL MEETINGS

In my judgment, smaller is better when it comes to truly productive meetings. Having said that, I should also add that, in postmeeting analysis, it is often difficult to put your finger on what made the small meeting better than its larger counterpart. Both share certain prerequisites, such as establishing a clear objective, considering nonmeeting alternatives, inviting the right people, and encouraging interactive participation on all sides. But there are some things that the small meeting doesn't have. The small meeting (of, say, eight or nine people) is by its nature less formal and more bent on being a shirt-sleeves working session. It often has no presentations and limited, if any, audiovisual aids. So where is the advantage?

The more casual atmosphere and fewer players improve communication. I've also noticed that energy is created because the sized-down meeting environment affords the manager other unique opportunities. Here are two examples:

■ *Priming the pump.* Dealing with a limited and manageable number of meeting invitees, the manager can jump-start the problem-solving process in a way that both helps people prepare for the meeting and serves as its action plan. You need only contact each participant (a brief e-mail will suffice) stating a bare-bones objective for the meeting and asking each to come prepared with three solutions to the particular problem faced. It may be something like, "What are your three suggestions for ways we can reduce operating costs during the next year?" or "Give me three ways we can increase production and still keep expenses at the current level."

The meeting then pretty much drives itself. To begin, you restate the problem to be solved, then systematically go through the various solutions offered. I suggest writing them on a board or flipchart (leave space between items, because similar or related answers will arise that can be grouped together as the discussion proceeds). In true brainstorming style we list all ideas first, without qualifying or rejecting any idea. When the suggestions have all been recorded, we go back and discuss each, airing reasons why we think a suggestion may or may not work. The final step in this phase is to rank or prioritize the viable answers.

This is a productive method that the manager can employ with a small meeting group, but one that would be logistically impractical with a larger group because of the sheer numbers of recommendations to be generated, reviewed, and recorded. It also induces the more timid member to play a part and gives the manager a number of options to examine.

■ *Keeping the meeting on time.* If everyday complaints about meetings are any barometer, it would seem that managers view shorter meetings as better meetings. We already know that the more people you invite, the longer the meeting becomes; therefore, smaller meetings equals shorter meetings equals better meetings.

In small and midsize meetings, you can effectively control the time in several ways. One of the best ways is to set a definite time limit and enforce it. When you announce the meeting, state both the starting time and the ending time or a "no later than" closing time. Tell participants that the meeting will "begin at 3:00 P.M. and end no later than 4:30 P.M." Or simply say that the meeting will run no more than ninety minutes. Obviously, you can't control the time if the meeting doesn't start on time, so set up your own rules to cover that circumstance. With a small meeting, you can be ruthless about starting on the dot if you wish to, but meeting leaders usually allow a little leeway if it's the boss or an important meeting participant that's missing. (In a larger meeting, there is more pressure to start on time because of the number of attendees you are immobilizing by waiting for some latecomer.)

I have heard time management professionals suggest scheduled meetings at odd hours—such as 9:10 instead of 9:00—to add a sense of urgency and specificity that ostensibly will get the attendees' attention and get them there on time. I haven't tried it, so I can't verify the effect, but I wouldn't hesitate to give it a try if I was experiencing persistent tardiness problems with meeting attendees.

MORE MEETING TIPS

Here is more food for thought for the meeting leader who wants to conduct more effective meetings in less time:

1. *Parliamentary, my dear Watson* . . . Before you scoff at *Robert's Rules of Order,* you might consider turning to it—or at least to its principles—to speed a meeting along. After all, parliamentary procedure was created to provide an orderly and systematic conduct of business discussions. Sounds like a meeting to me. It did in 1876, too, when Major Henry Robert, a U.S. army engineer, adopted this method to conduct his church business meetings. Admittedly, the language is too stilted and the procedure too stiff and cumbersome to overlay on most company business

meetings, large or small, but there are some applicable lessons for meeting leaders:

■ *Control.* Being able to follow some established rule for gaining the floor, rather than having meeting attendees interrupting one another, is certainly desirable. The manager, as meeting leader, must exercise forceful governance to maintain order with a word, look, and gesture rather than a gavel.

■ *Organization.* Under parliamentary rules, presenting matters in an orderly and logical sequence (i.e., minutes, reports, unfinished business, new business) provided a necessary structure and sequence for addressing business matters. As the meeting leader, you must likewise have a clear idea of where the meeting is going and provide structure if time is to be managed wisely.

■ *Decision Making.* In a word, vote! You can expedite decision making in your meetings by putting any measure to a vote. Although you'll never actually use this parliamentary terminology, know the difference between *majority* and *plurality* and always allow for a negative "those opposed" vote. Don't leave a meeting in limbo when you could have asked participants for their views. Always complete the process by announcing the result. No one should leave your meeting not knowing what was decided.

2. *Other encounters you can expect.* One is a threat, the other harmless, but both of these participants can usurp valuable meeting time, so at least be aware of them.

■ *The Monopolizer.* The monopolizer wants to take over. Remind yourself that this is not his or her meeting. You can divert a wayward outburst or grab for attention by saying something like, "Just hold that thought. Right now we're discussing . . . ," or "That's good input, but that's not the real issue at the moment," or "Okay, let's hear another opinion on this now." You can be a good listener up to a point because you know you need to let the person express an opinion even if you don't agree with it. But you must not relinquish control of the meeting. If the monopolizer is interrupting, sometimes you can simply raise your hand, or speak louder, and the person will back off.

■ *The Compulsive Contributor.* It goes with the territory, and is more an observation than a caution, but almost every meeting of any size includes at least one person who feels compelled to make a statement—not to shed light on the subject, but to shed light on his or her presence at the meeting. These participants don't want to just sit there quietly because that could indicate that they didn't understand the discussion or had nothing to contribute (which may be the case). So they strain mightily to construct a comment that validates their participation and grasp of the topic. Let's not get too sanctimonius—we've probably all done it at one time or another. It smacks of insecurity, but it doesn't bog down the meeting unless there are several people trying to weigh in on each point. It even adds a little humor, particularly when a compulsive contributor has spent fifteen minutes mentally crafting a cogent point that he is ready to make, only to have another participant eloquently make the same point only seconds before.

3. *Saving information: to find it, bind it!* Meetings run on information, and if it's not readily available, precious

time is wasted and irretrievably lost. You can't prevent
others from dropping the ball, but you can make sure
that *you* have the facts and figures required and can
find them when needed. It goes back to how you
captured and organized the information in the first
place. To be prepared for any meeting, even on short
notice, I favor one self-contained source of
information that is readily available to any manager.

■ *The Three-Ring Binder.* There are plenty of ways to
file information—in your PC, in file folders, in a
file cabinet, or in a shoe box. In my experience,
though, there is certain information you will wish
to retain in hard copy in a more organized manner.
For those instances, my motto is "to find it, bind
it": Build three-ring binders for ongoing activities
like regular standing committees, clubs, boards,
and foundations, and special projects that generate
a lot of paperwork and a lot of meetings. That
binder will come in handy for organizing and
retaining the material but is even more reassuring
when it's tucked under your arm on the way to
your meeting. When business is being conducted,
you can quickly locate previous minutes, letters, or
the budget instead of shuffling through an
unorganized file folder. It may even be so well
arranged that, in an emergency, someone else can
grab the binder and go in your stead!

Set up the dividers in whatever way works best
for you. You can even stick an index page in the
front, just to remind yourself what's located where.
Or save time with a set of commercially available
colored, numbered dividers that includes a color-
coded index page so you can simply fill in the
blanks. If the activity covered is new to you, or
outside the company, sometimes it's a good idea to

begin your binder with a "Who's Who" page so you have ready reference to names and contact numbers of the key players. Then set up typical dividers for programs or projects covered, correspondence, meeting minutes, budget and financial statements, legal (contracts and rules), etc. Reminder: After each meeting, punch papers that aren't already three-hole drilled and update the binder. Final disposition: Set up binders by year, and keep them on the shelf for as long as you feel they may be of value.

EFFECTIVE USE OF VISUAL AIDS

Visual aids and props can be the greatest thing that ever happened to your meeting, or they can be the worst. If they are poor or misused, they can let the air out of a presentation in a hurry. Most of today's visual aids are generated by laptop computers, and new presentation technology can simplify the production process and give you very impressive results. But whether using Microsoft PowerPoint, Web-conferencing tools, electronic whiteboards, or plain old flipcharts, the rule of the game is the same: Don't let the medium become the message. Determine the purpose of the presentation before you begin to add bells and whistles.

I am no technical expert on great audiovisuals, but I know one when I see one, and I know the few simple things that a manager needs to know to employ visual aids successfully. Audiovisual aids exist for five reasons:

- To clarify (i.e., to explain complex things that words alone cannot)
- To dramatize (i.e., to reveal something that stirs emotions)

- To emphasize (i.e., to repeat or enhance the importance)
- To reinforce (i.e., to illustrate a key point in another medium)
- To review (i.e., to wrap up, usually at the end of the presentation)

If you can't justify them according to one or more of these criteria, don't use them.

I also know the starting point, the environment in which visual aids will be used. You want a well-lit room for every other aspect of the meeting, but you want a suitably darkened room to enhance on screen projections, slides, and transparencies. It doesn't have to be darkened completely—just light enough for you to be able to see and for the audience to be able to take notes. I once attended a midday presentation at a modern law university conference room. The room was magnificent for various reports being made, but the meeting closed with a slide presentation that was disastrous. What made the room so great earlier was its full ceiling skylight, but there was no simple way that such ambient light could be screened to darken the room. Many so-called multipurpose rooms are not really suited to handling multiple presentations.

> Visual aids should complement the speaker's remarks, not become the whole presentation.

Use a visual aid to complement the speaker, not to cause the audience to divide its attention between the speaker and the visual aid. When speakers use a projection in place of notes, they are expecting the visual to keep them on track. When they also use a slide that contains a lot of words, they are expecting the slide to make their presentation for them.

The visual may reinforce the message being presented, high-light key points that require emphasis, and clarify a concept, but it should not become the total presentation.

A visual can explain things for you, so don't distract the viewer by talking all the way through it. You don't need to read aloud what the viewer is reading.

Walk that important line between keeping the visuals consistent, so that they look as if they came from the same person or the same company, and using some variety, includ-ing a reasonable amount of different graphics in pictures, headlines, charts, and graphs. Don't swamp the presentation with too many different typefaces, however.

Don't expect the visual aid to accomplish more than is possible in explaining complex technical subjects, either. If the topic is loaded with technology and incorporates multiple steps, distribute a handout instead.

When using slides, allow the audience a few seconds to view the slide before you start talking about it. Ordinarily, it's a good idea to use only one slide for each idea and one picture per slide. Don't make it difficult for the viewer to figure out.

When you've covered the slide adequately in your pre-sentation, change it. It's disconcerting to audience members for you to be off on another subject when their attention is still focused on the old slide. Change slides quickly, without awkward pauses. If you have someone operating the projector for you, work out a subtle signal between the two of you—anything to avoid the "Next slide, please" signal.

If you use a flipchart, place it in a corner of the room, not right in the center. Decide whether you want to prepare pages in advance and uncover them as you go along, or whether you want to develop the chart on the spot. If you do the latter, print your text by hand in large letters, and use all capital letters unless your caps and lowercase writing is respectable. Write only the keywords and abbreviate as much as possible without losing meaning. I've also found it extremely helpful to pencil in any private notes to yourself, lightly, in the margins of the page.

When you speak, stand to the side and face the audience—and don't speak to the audience while you are still writing.

The best visual aid of all is an object. If you can present an actual sample of something, preferably an object that can be shown and then passed around the room, you will add a memorable impression.

You can leave a lasting impression, too, by printing out copies of slides and distributing them at the end of the meeting as a take-away. Some presenters working to an audience with a high-quality flipchart have created miniature flipcharts as a nice memento for participants.

Above all, you get a good presentation in the same way you get to Carnegie Hall: Practice, practice, practice.

OTHER MEETING ROOM CONSIDERATIONS

I have always been the first person to arrive at the meeting room. That may not sound like a smart use of the manager's time, but I have often been glad I did it—often enough that I wouldn't have it any other way. I need to know that the room is set up the way that it is supposed to be. I want to familiarize myself with the room itself, know where the air-conditioning or heating controls are, and where the light switches and sound controls are (and who will be responsible for controlling them). I want to do a sound check on the microphone and I want to know where the rest rooms are located.

If this meeting is off-site at a hotel, I want to know what other meetings are going on and who's booked next door. (That's because I once conducted a professional society meeting in a room separated only by a too-thin folding partition from a mind-numbing labor union dance.) Sometimes even sheer coincidence can raise its ugly head: I spoke at an Association of Industrial Advertisers luncheon meeting at an Anaheim, California, hotel—the same day as an American Institute of Architects scheduled a luncheon next door in the same hotel at the same hour. The meeting was delayed twenty minutes while we sorted out AIA advertisers from AIA architects.

What About Refreshments?

It is always a good idea to have coffee, tea, and cold drinks in the back of the room—and ice water on the tables. Likewise, cookies or muffins are a welcome treat. Often Danish pastries are more than one person may want and should be cut in half beforehand. I'm ambivalent about continental breakfasts, fruit bowls, and other offerings as a kick-start to a morning meeting and generally question the value. Maybe it's the nuisance factor or maybe it's the unwelcome sight of so much food often going unused.

USE THE MEETING AS A REWARD: AN EXAMPLE

Occasionally you will be responsible for a meeting that you want to make a special event. One such regularly scheduled meeting I convened each year was the annual Beckman communications management meeting that included communication managers from each operating division throughout the United States, selected managers from our international business units, and key executives from the corporate communications department and our outside advertising agency. (During the SmithKline Beckman years, I also invited representatives from SmithKline so that the Philadelphia parents would know what was going on.) The meeting's primary business objectives were to coordinate activities between businesss units, develop and communicate corporate policy, make decisions on advertising campaigns and other media programs, and update middle-level managers on top management's strategic plans. (It was not unusual for the CEO or other brass to address the group.) Usually fifteen to twenty people attended this meeting.

In addition to those objectives, there was another one I had in mind—recognition for exceptional effort. It required a modest investment to make this a rewarding and enjoyable experience for our communication managers, something they would look forward to rather than just see as another obligation. But that investment was well worthwhile and certainly commensurate with the multimillion-dollar program and budget investments carried by the invitees. As a result, this became a very popular meeting and one to which even visiting speakers looked forward. I enter it into evidence only because it encompassed several key elements of the ideal meeting:

- *Site.* Although some meetings were held on-site at the company office, most were scheduled in hotel or resort facilities in the area. This afforded a change of scene for the participants, removing them from the ebb and flow of the office, yet the site was always within the driving range of company speakers invited for special presentations.

- *Duration.* Meetings were typically two to two-and-a-half days in length. A meeting would begin on a Wednesday morning, for instance, with attendees having arrived on Tuesday night and generally mixing informally that evening. On several occasions, we had a golf tournament or other activity on the day preceding the meeting's opening. The program ran (on schedule, I might add) throughout the day

Wednesday, with free time Wednesday evening. The program resumed on Thursday morning and shut down early Thursday afternoon before a Thursday evening dinner and program. On Friday, we began early but concluded before lunch so out-of-towners could make their flights.

■ *Agenda.* The agenda was balanced, with formal presentations intermixed with interactive sessions. All were controlled to stay within the time parameters, and any unfinished discussions were assigned for further study or carried over to free time later in the meeting. There was also a varied menu of inside-company speakers and outside experts, which kept the program interesting and brought in fresh points of view.

■ *Recognition.* I mentioned recognition as one of the objectives. This materialized in two ways. During the opening day, communication managers reviewed efforts of the past twelve months and previewed their new campaigns and programs, affording them an opportunity to take a bow for their best creative work. At the final day's dinner (sometimes called "The Last Supper"), I also presented awards and recognition to those with especially outstanding accomplishments.

■ *Special Guests.* In a sense, most of our speakers from outside the department were VIPs—either recognized experts in their field or key executives within the corporation. We went them one better, though, in the closing dinner by bringing in nationally known inspirational speakers that even the VIPs wanted to hear. The bottom line was that the dinners were always enjoyable and all attendees felt like the honored guests that they were.

■ *Visual Aids.* Throughout the meeting, the whole gamut of visual aids was used, and an audiovisual professional assisted with video, slides, film, flipcharts, or whatever other materials were needed. Presenters knew what was expected and were usually well prepared.

■ *Cost.* The visiting managers were responsible for their own lodging and travel, with the exception of international visitors, whom we assisted with both lodging and travel. The company bore the expense of all meals and other meeting costs. Speakers were paid for by the company or subsidized by our advertising agency.

All in all, this series of meetings over more than twenty years came as close as I've seen to the ideal meeting of its type.

OTHER TIPS TO SAVE MEETING TIME

There are other things you can do to streamline your meetings and save time. For example:

1. *Structure your agenda in a logical sequence.* If item D will include discussion that has a substantial influence on item C, then obviously D should precede C. To do otherwise is to spend time on issues that are premature and invite needless repetition.

2. *Keep everyone informed of the basics.* If the meeting is held off-site, or if visitors from outside your work group are attending, let people know where to find the rest rooms, telephones, and the nearest fax or copy machine at the start of the meeting.

3. *Don't turn the meeting room into a telephone booth.* If at all possible, have folks leave their cell phones outside. If an assistant is taking calls for participants, have him or her hold calls until the next break and

distribute phone slips then. Urgent phone messages should be brought to someone near the door who can distribute them discreetly.

4. *Use a flip chart to record key ideas and make them visible to everyone at the meeting.* Tear off pages and tape them (with masking tape) on the walls so that they remain visible for reference throughout the entire session.

5. *Appoint a facilitator who keeps the meeting moving, keeps an eye on the clock, and acts as recorder.* To save time, record only decisions. If the meeting absolutely requires detailed minutes, then keep them brief, underline action items and responsible individuals, and distribute them within a few days of the meeting. I always tried to get published minutes out the door within twenty-four hours and found it was much appreciated by the participants.

KEEP BIG MEETINGS PROFESSIONAL

While the large event meetings are outside the purview of this chapter, even a ten- to twenty-person affair is capable of self-destruction. When the meeting gets too large or is moved off-site, detail begins to wag the dog. The manager's objectives and simple plan may be held hostage while sensitive details are shuffled about with audiovisual people, meeting planners, or hotel or resort staff. You have reason to be very wary, though, of a worse accident waiting to happen: giving a well-meaning but inexperienced person responsibility for a large meeting off-site. Then the wisdom rings out in the old saying, "Lord, preserve us from the gifted amateur." It's a job for a professional. The ideal governance is for the event to be handled by an experienced company person or by the outside professional staff, but under the watchful eye of a competent company person.

Large meetings may mean inviting outside speakers. In this event, I have another rule: Never book a speaker that you haven't heard or who doesn't come with a strong recommendation from someone whose opinion you highly respect. There have been too many disasters involving decent people who either didn't have anything to say or had a lot to say but didn't know how to say it.

KEEP SMALL MEETINGS SMALL

We said at the outset that one-on-one meetings don't count as meetings. Nevertheless, there are some actions you can take for even these encounters that will save you time. Suppose, for instance, you get a call from another manager within the company who urgently wants to meet on a specific topic. The topic is one that doesn't appear to require access to your files and is unlikely to require calling additional staff members into an expanded session. One option you can exercise is to offer to come to the other manager's office. Why? Because then you can control the time and leave when you want to, avoiding the possibility of being trapped in your office for the rest of the afternoon. Also, if you truly want to be accommodating, you know that the other manager may be more comfortable on her own turf and it will probably be a better meeting. After all, we spend enough time in our home office environments, so it isn't going to hurt to give it up now and then.

Here's a final number for you—zero. That's the number of times that meeting responsibilities are mentioned in any manager's position description. You can add a zero as well for the amount of hours spent in your academic courses or in your company orientation on planning and conducting meetings. That would seem to be a glaring oversight if we are expected to live about a quarter of our management life in meetings.

8

MANAGING
YOUR REPUTATION

It is a luxury to be understood.

—*Ralph Waldo Emerson*

The great monumental structures of ancient Greece, like the Parthenon, are said to be ones that were created with a 360-degree perspective. The building, viewed from any angle, presented the same consistent character and identity. Wouldn't you want your personal and managerial qualities expressed the same way? That's reason enough to be your own press agent. Some will reject the notion, saying, "I am not interested in having a public relations image." Trouble is, you have one whether you want one or not. The question is only whether you want to participate in shaping it.

Corporations call it image. You can call it reputation. But don't call it bragging or egotism. Making an honest effort to ensure that your personal contribution is duly recognized is simply called common sense. That conclusion would be a little more evident were we not burdened with the puritan ethic that one shouldn't draw attention to his or her own exploits and that recognition will come in due time. Granted, the amount of effort devoted to personal publicity should be held in proper check, but subtle promotion of yourself is not a totally self-centered exercise. It is closely linked with the promotion of your business team and benefits other individuals within the department, as well as the whole enterprise.

If you're uncomfortable being your own press agent, you might instead view it as an opportunity to correct any misinformation that may be out there. For instance, you may wish to correct wayward impressions that suggest you are "difficult to work with" when it really means that you are a stickler for doing the job right. Your boss needs the latter view. However you choose to view the management of your reputation, it goes with the territory and is an important step in your career ladder.

PUTTING YOUR TRUE CHARACTER IN FOCUS

I have always highly valued corporate identity in its truest sense but disdained the term "corporate image" because it sounded too much like something done with smoke and mirrors. Actually, all we want to accomplish, with the company's identity as with yours, is to make your true character visible. That can be done with a modest but continuous effort in four ways:

1. Assess the product (you) and the way it is packaged.
2. Ascertain what style changes would be prudent.
3. Decide who needs to know more about your accomplishments.
4. Determine how that should be communicated.

Look at Yourself

I don't mean your physical appearance, although if it is presentable and pleasing, you already have an advantage. No, I'm talking about a picture of your present status in the organization. A little soul searching is incredibly beneficial because it identifies areas of concern that you should be addressing anyway.

> A little soul searching can identify areas of concern.

Look first at where you are positioned within the company vis-à-vis other managers and how visible you are within the management ranks. Do upper levels of management know who you are and what you do? Do you have a support base of friends and associates whom you can count on for loyalty? Do you consider yourself to be confident and to have a pleasing personality? How do you think you are perceived by others—as an up-and-coming executive or as just another employee? Does this public perception accurately reflect your skills and output? Don't feel guilty if it does and you have self-doubt about whether you are management material at all. You can still find happiness and fulfillment as a specialist in a field that you truly enjoy. If, however, you feel that you have the right combination of management skills but that they are just not adequately being communicated, then we have work to do.

We all have some idea about what a management style is, and you will have a sense of what the existing culture is for your company. If your natural style is radically different from the company culture and that of your colleagues, then you can expect to encounter some hostility in fitting in. If that is the case, you may be in the wrong company and should look for a more hospitable environment. (Don't jettison all your individuality, though, just to conform to an uncomfortable role. Remember that the only thing that may conveniently fit into a pigeonhole is a pigeon.)

Who Needs to Know?

Assuming that your style is not out of sync with the company style, your next assignment is to decide who the key players are who need to be influenced. Peter Drucker encapsulated this best in the "Effective Executive" film series with this quote: "Who in this company has to know what I am doing, and in what form do I have to present it so that he can understand it and use it to make himself a more effective executive?" It would be a good idea to copy this and keep it next to your desk. Who needs to know you better?

You may want to start with a piece of paper and draw circles connecting yourself with your boss (the one who measures your performance), as well as filling in the various people who have ongoing business dealings with you. Some would appear on a normal organizational chart, but others may be more informal connections that are no less important. You may have no direct reporting relationship with the chief financial officer, yet the CFO's image of you as a responsible administrator of the company funds that you control can have far-reaching consequences.

SEVEN KEYS TO IMPROVING YOUR IMAGE AND REPUTATION

There are a couple of ways you can approach reputation building. One is by direct impression, which is derived from face-to-face contact with people and their experiences with you. In other words, it is how you build personal relationships one at a time. Another is through image. This is created by people who may not actually know you but have heard about you (perhaps heard about you *from* you, without knowing it). Both approaches are important and both should be consistent. I've listed seven practices that are instrumental in influencing direct impressions with your coworkers and bosses, as well as providing fodder for the image-building apparatus. The net result is your most important asset—a positive reputation.

1. *Look the part.* If you want to play the part, look the part. It's no surprise that unconventional hair, tattoos, unusual beards and mustaches, and eccentric clothing have derailed many a business career. If you're in a management environment where none of that matters, consider yourself exceptional. If you're not, try paying more attention to a professional business management appearance and good grooming. Invest in some new clothes. A wardrobe made up of a few quality pieces will work better than a lot of bargain-

basement items. Executive recruiters say the road to success in a business environment is greatly enhanced with a well-tailored suit and complementary blouse or shirt. Polished shoes help, too. If you are in a business that has standards for dress (the military, for instance), then follow those religiously. If you're in a profession that is characterized by more casual attire, quality and good taste are still requisites.

2. *Network for success.* Network like crazy! Go to every business meeting, professional society meeting, conference, and trade show that you can. Meet people who have similar interests and who may be able to influence your career. The contacts are valuable and you never know just when and how they will pay off. Salespeople are masters at it and build a network of acquaintances and customers that provides a line of communication into every account throughout their territory.

   Some people network effectively until they reach the management ranks, but thereafter seem to retreat behind their walls. Networking is valuable at any stage of your career and is different from building a support system. The network is essentially a communications system and is composed of contacts rather than loyal allies. These contacts are almost as valuable because they can provide essential information about who's doing what and the environment outside as well as inside your business. Incidentally, one of the people who can be most helpful to your career is your boss's assistant. Assistants frequently have a lot of influence, so you should go out of your way to be friendly and cooperative with these contacts.

3. *Develop a specialty.* Carve out a unique niche for yourself. Specialize in something and become an

expert in it. Become your company's focal point in that area. Study it, research it, and know more about that topic than anyone else in your area. It may be an expertise you already have—for example, you may be multilingual or have special knowledge in international relations, age and sex discrimination, government contracts, production control, environmental impacts, or the Internet. You have something that can enhance your reputation.

Now find a way to apply that expert knowledge, possibly by volunteering for an assignment or getting on a committee. I chaired the corporate trademark and graphics council and was able to become a very visible conduit for that type of information throughout the company. When I became a member of the corporation's historical committee, and later its chair, I found myself working closely with the company's founder, the CEO, and with many members of the president's staff—all of whom were invaluable contacts. Other committee tasks built bridges into other segments of the corporation. Don't avoid them. Become an expert in some erudite subject and you can almost (I stress almost) become indispensable.

4. *Show that you're informed.* If you read a lot, then you are going to run across good business information. Most of it will show up in newspapers, business magazines, and trade papers. Become an informal clipping service and send clips of interest to other managers. I even created a little notepad-size transmittal form with a tire track across it and the message: "Here's something I ran across that may be of interest to you." The results are heartwarming. You accomplish several things. First, you really do provide a worthwhile information service for the people to

whom you send these notices. Second, you convince people that you're a person who is committed to the business and not just spending your evenings on the couch. Third, you are seeing to it that words like "expert" and "well informed" are associated with you and your reputation.

5. *Be active in a professional society or association.* Notice that I didn't just say join a professional association. In our company, I was happy to approve membership dues, meeting costs, and expense accounts for those who actively participated in societies and associations. I found these activities to be invaluable for myself and the staff as a way to pursue continuing education and to network, recruit new employees, and just create good friendships. It's also a way of putting something back into the pot—giving a little back to whatever profession you're pursuing. I attended every meeting and seminar I possibly could and always took notes when anything was said that I wanted to capture. Such activities may consume a lot of your time, but I still encourage the young manager to join, participate, volunteer for committees, and hold an office. It will add to your reputation inside the company and provide valuable exposure and contacts outside the company. And it's a nice reflection on the employer when an employee is an officer of the local professional association.

6. *Celebrate successes in print.* Create your own vehicle for spreading the good news about your department's exploits. You needn't turn the spotlight on yourself—and you shouldn't, since you are the issuing authority. But you can show by example that you're leading a first-rate team that is doing good things for the company. I prefer a one-page newsletter or cover

letter that highlights a noteworthy accomplishment of the group. A typical format would state a problem and show its solution. Concentrate on the specifics of the solution without lacing the story with lavish praise. The point is to provide nice recognition for your people and subliminally let other managers know that you're doing a quality management job. In a multidivisional company, such news items also plug divisions into what their counterparts elsewhere are doing.

Although publish or perish may not apply to your position, maybe publish and flourish does apply. How about enhancing your stature in the company by writing an article for a trade magazine or other publication? There's plenty of help available on style and even guidance on what to write about. The media has an insatiable appetite for material and you just may be able to benefit from it.

7. *Make alliances in high places.* You probably discovered during your first days as a manager that life is easier when you have a supportive boss or well-placed supportive friends. Therein lies one of the cardinal truths of business: Since you cannot personally control everything that happens to you in business, you had best establish positive relationships with those who do. I refer to those vital few who will be making decisions that affect your career. Your boss is one, of course, as well as the personnel manager and other executives, peers, and even subordinates who populate your corner of the business world. Some make decisions; others influence decisions. Either way, you must forge a critical link with these people and then service it rigorously with direct, personal contact.

Even senior managers have confided that they

wish they'd developed those relationships earlier in their career. Corporate public relations practitioners have a saying: "The time to make friends is before you need them." You can't suddenly start currying favor when you're in trouble. Personal public relations should be treated the same way. It's crucial that you build a strong support base and that it be started as soon as possible. Too many young managers have set sail in business with a thin or limited base, counting on a few friends from college or the community. You need to create loyal allies in your business group (the higher up the better). The way to make a friend is to be a good friend. Look for ways to sincerely contribute to that person's success. Go out of your way to help in difficult times of need.

Caution: Once you have a good relationship, you don't want to overuse those alliances. You have to keep the account balanced, too. When you take a favor from a friend, you need to return the favor at your earliest opportunity.

> Establish positive relationships and create loyal allies, the higher up the better.

Most important, don't let alliances lapse. Don't let them fall into neglect, or they won't be there when you need them. To keep the alliance activated, you must keep in touch. Face-to-face personal contact is best, but a short note can work wonders, too. It can be business related or just a note to say "Congratulations on your win at the summer tennis tournament." Ideally it should be hand written and dispatched promptly, not two weeks later.

A brief phone call is also helpful. Sometimes we neglect to give a colleague a call because we think we don't have anything important to report. That may be the best time to call, just to show that you care and are interested in what's going on in that person's life. Even if you don't have a pressing reason to call, maybe the other person has something he or she needs to share with you. Ask yourself, Who should I call today?

There you have it—a seven-step insurance policy to protect your image. According to Lee Iacocca, success comes not from what you know, but from whom you know and how you present yourself to those people. Being a good press agent for yourself goes a long way toward meeting those requirements

MANAGING CHANGE, CHALLENGES, CONFLICTS, AND CRISES

If we had no winter, the spring would not be so pleasant:
If we did not sometimes taste adversity,
prosperity would not be so welcome.

—CHARLOTTE BRONTË

If you are one of those managers who seeks to avoid trouble at any cost, you may wish to skip this chapter. It will not be so easy in your business, though, to skip the real-life events covered here. Managers can expect to encounter distressing and difficult predicaments in the normal course of commerce and they cannot be brushed aside lightly. Remember these words of advice: When we lose sight of what is utterly essential, we will only do what is important. Handling the issues of change, challenges, conflicts, and crises is utterly essential, and managing these circumstances is far more critical than what we previously thought was merely important.

Throughout many of the preceding chapters, we've covered the mountain highs of management—helping people develop, reclaiming wasted time, uncovering ways to make your work more efficient and more effective. Unfortunately, part of the manager's job is also to go down into the valley and face challenges, and sometimes to go look for them and wrestle them to the ground before they become major issues. The most obvious reason many managers shrink from this mission is that it forces them out of a comfort zone.

To me, the whole secret in dealing with management trials and tribulations lies in your attitude toward them. If you avoid conflict altogether, or deny that it exists, then it already has a big advantage over you. If you face up to it, you have an even chance. If, on the other hand, you expect it and accept it freely as an essential part of your responsibility, the advantage swings to you. Success goes to the prepared.

The best advice I've heard comes from a Marine sergeant, a veteran night combat instructor with the USMC boot camp at Parris Island, South Carolina. He is conducting training—facing a group of recruits huddled in a ravine on a pitch black, moonless night when you can't see your hand in front of your face. "You're afraid of the dark." he says. "That's okay, because I am going to teach you how to live in the dark, so you won't be afraid of it anymore." He proceeds to teach and guide and counsel until the recruits not only feel comfortable in the darkness, but feel they belong there and now have an advantage over others in the darkness.

Facing challenges and conflicts may never become your favorite pastime, but you can grow to accept them as an essential part of the job, unintimidated and actually looking forward to disarming difficulties and reaching a happy resolution.

CORRALLING THE FOUR HORSEMEN

The most common threats to your company's tranquility come from four sources, and they may occur independently or as part of a progression of events:

- *Change.* Although change is constantly going on in business, any variation in the organization or "the way we do things around here" will seem disruptive and threatening to some employees.

- *Challenges.* Challenges are those conditions that have the potential for negative impact if left unresolved and that likely will not be resolved without management's intervention. Challenges involve conditions usually within your normal job responsibilities.

- *Conflicts.* More specific disputes—sometimes disagreements pitting employee against employee or employee against boss—are often surrounded with tension and hostility. Conflicts involve people.

■ *Crises.* A crisis is any unexpected event that has the potential for serious adverse, and perhaps catastrophic, effect upon the company, its reputation, or its employees.

Although this fearsome foursome is unlikely to appear in a sequence, it is not impossible. For instance, a hypothetical case may begin with a fairly simple change: a company downsizing and facility relocation in which one business unit is relegated to 30 percent smaller space. This results in a challenging situation that requires reducing common work areas so as to maintain most office and work spaces, sharing some facilities and certain support functions with another department, and even changing working hours to permit full utilization of equipment. This upset leads to complaints of favoritism and several escalating conflicts between employees and even threats of violence, which attracts labor union attention, triggers grievance procedures and unwanted media attention, and becomes a budding crisis situation.

In each instance, the prescribed answer is planning and preparation beforehand, rapid response, cool heads prevailing when the stuff hits the fan, and follow-up action to lessen the chances of the problem recurring. Here's a quick take on some of the issues in keeping change, challenge, conflict, and crisis inside the pen.

MEETING CHANGE HEAD-ON

Most people don't welcome change. Even managers, who are agents of change and fond of saying "the only constant around here is change," are reticent about embracing it. That's unproductive, because change constantly happens in the workplace and we had better be ready to adapt to it and use it to our advantage. In business, change is what keeps us moving ahead. The effects are unsettling, but they don't have to be negative. Most change is for the better. Some change isn't change at all, but history repeating itself. (For instance, e-commerce is reinventing commercial practices—like bartering—that are thousands of years old.)

> We had better be ready to accept change and use it to our advantage.

When addressing the problems associated with change, first make sure that you are not one of the problems. As the manager, be certain that you're not guilty of initiating unwarranted change, such as regularly reorganizing the department's structure. Obviously, your staff would prefer a measure of stability and the opportunity to digest one major upheaval before you announce the next one. Realignment is natural as the organization grows, and a restructure can improve efficiency and inject some excitement into the business. Although redrawing reporting lines on the organizational chart may be simple for the manager, it is not so simple for those affected.

In 210 B.C., Roman critic Petronius Arbiter observed, "We trained hard, but it seemed that every time we were beginning to form up into teams, we would be reorganized. I was to learn later in life that we tend to meet any new situation by reorganizing; and a wonderful method it can be for creating the illusion of progress while producing confusion, inefficiency, and demoralization." The moral is: Don't shuffle the deck to respond to a minor or temporary situation. Make fewer and deeper changes if you want to maintain momentum for your organization's progress.

Gradual, expected change—whether in mission, structure, or process—is not a problem. Most of us accept that as a given in a progressive company. But when you or your employees come face to face with unexpected change, there is often resistance to letting go of the familiar. Even without recognizing it, those affected begin putting up barriers to change. It is your job as manager to explain the change (as far in advance as possible), to address concerns head-on, and to work through it with people who are worried because their routines and lives are being transformed.

Change may materialize in many ways—a downsizing, a transfer to another department, a company reorganization or merger, a relocation, or any drastic change in methods and procedures. Each is different in impact, but each has in it similar scenarios, and each can be managed. Here are four basic steps to managing change:

1. *Put the cards on the table.* And the sooner the better. Employees can smell out the fact that change is in the wind. Don't try to hide it, unless there is some overpowering reason for confidentiality. The sooner you can open up with your staff and answer all their questions, the better it is for their peace of mind—and for their confidence in your leadership. Be fully prepared with all the reasons to support why this change is necessary. Anticipate their questions and fears. In this stage of disclosure, keep the discussion calm, objective, and factual.

2. *Consider the emotional factors.* Okay, you've laid out the objective rationale for the change. Now you must turn your attention to the emotional, human side of the situation. For the employee, this is not an exercise in logic. For many, it suggests disruption and abandoning some security and comfort that is near and dear to them. Be an understanding listener, and be patient. It will take some time, and there is a sort of grieving and adjustment experience employees will

go through. Your attitude will set the tone and make acceptance easier.

3. *Get employees involved in the process.* Encourage your staff to find ways to deal with the change. This means letting them find the positives in the change. Evaluate as many options as possible. It means giving employees a sense of ownership of the change itself and letting them see that they have not given up control over the situation. Help them get over the uncertainty by demonstrating the possible benefits of change. Sure, losing jobs and coworkers is painful, but the loss can improve stability and competitiveness, which will protect jobs for many others. Sure, the new methods are demanding, but they represent a fresh opportunity for growth and development. While you're encouraging input, remember that the employee is making some big changes and compromises. Be prepared to make some compromises, too.

4. *Refocus.* After you've allowed a reasonable time to adjust, it's time to refocus on the new order that is in place. Get people thinking about new goals and new ways of doing things. Make the necessary adaptations to create an exciting work environment that is as supportive as the old one was. If there are still some workers who are negative, or whose attitude and work have deteriorated, have a private session with each individual. Be understanding, but make it clear that the train is about to leave the station. It's time to move on!

TAKING ON CHALLENGES

In the manager's vernacular, challenges are not unexpected winds that suddenly blow down the door. Instead, they are a fairly obvious part of the job that just happens to be loaded with a not-so-obvious potential for trouble. Common challenges faced by the manager are:

■ *Budget battles.* The budgeting process is generally not considered a challenge, but it has all the necessary components. Even building a budget can be challenging because it presents difficult decisions on where to allocate sometimes-stretched resources. When it comes down to which horse to bet on, and which constituency to fund, there are pressures aplenty. Even more stressful is the budget cut, when both programs and people are at stake.

■ *Turf disagreements.* From time to time, managers disagree on who should have the responsibility for a certain function or work group. This straddles the fence between conflict and challenge and moves to the conflict side if it tends to be very personal between the managers involved. Ordinarily, you are dealing with a philosophical rather than a personal difference, but an intense one nevertheless.

■ *The barrier reef.* Barriers are limits or obstructions that pose a challenge for the new manager. Some are artificial, most are temporary, and even a few are too many. There is sometimes an acceptance barrier imposed by an older manager who expects the newcomer to first prove worthy of the "good ol' boys" or "good ol' girls" club. Or the bias mentality that questions whether this is a job for a woman, or a minority. Any barrier that denies the new manager full access to information or the tools to do the job is, at that moment, a serious challenge.

■ *Enforcing employment policies.* Even for the seasoned manager, employment issues are high on the list of challenges to face. Those dealing with hiring are not much of a problem, but the policing of rules about attendance, punctuality, dress, and demeanor takes its toll. Then we come to reprimands and disciplinary action, and the distasteful task of firing the unproductive employee.

■ *Terminating the problem employee.* I hesitate to add more gravity to this issue because managers already treat it like a harrowing near-death experience. It ordinarily isn't even an unexpected event. If it is, then either the employee missed some warning signals or the signaling device (i.e., the manager) was not functioning. Sometimes the worker leaves an employer no choice but to fire him. If the employer-employee personal communications were in operating order, we might avoid such surprises. Of all the personnel crises that managers face, this is the one in which the manager should be in closest contact with professional human resources representation. In a good company, human resources will have someone well versed in what to do in these difficult situations.

CASE <u>STUDY</u>:

THE CHALLENGE OF TERMINATING AN EMPLOYEE

The biggest mistake a manager can make is hiring—or keeping—the wrong employee. If you made the first mistake, then don't compound it by making the second as well. Keeping a marginal or unproductive employee can do damage to the morale of the whole department. It even does a disservice to the malingering employee, because it gives the impression that a poor level of work is acceptable. Taking decisive action can benefit failing employees by redirecting them to another specialty where they will be more proficient. (This was evident when I terminated a young advertising assistant who, it turned out, really wanted to be a woodworker. How he had ended up in the communications business, I'll never know—but I do know he was relieved to be cut loose. I had no doubt that the world needs good woodworkers more than it needs poor communicators.)

> Keeping a poor performer can damage the whole department.

I am not suggesting that managers should treat termination lightly, and I align myself with those who strongly view termination as an act of last resort. Managers all hope that subtle disciplinary action will resolve most employee shortcomings and that more severe disciplinary action can be avoided except in rare cases. We hope, too, that discussions and warnings will lead to a remedy, since the real purpose of disciplinary action is correction, not punishment.

Too often, though, the manager neglects to connect with the failing employee and the problems and consequences are not discussed until the situation is almost beyond repair. That is a shame and a loss for the company, as well as the terminated employee. Given a choice, the company would prefer to spend money on

retaining happy employees rather than sup-
porting headhunters.

The Difficult and the Allowable

Managers usually don't encounter much
resistance when terminating employees due to
business doldrums. Workers know they aren't
guaranteed a job, and they know that anybody—including the company president—can
go when times turn sour. It's not as clear when
the cuts are due to management changes or a
position that has unexpectedly been abolished.

The truly challenging times for a manager
come when the termination is for poor performance or various types of misconduct. It is absolutely critical to consult with your company's
human resources department before initiating a
termination to make sure that you are acting in
accord with the many laws and regulations
designed to protect employees. This is particularly true if the person being fired is a member
of a minority group, a woman, or an older employee. If you fire an employee without care for
these legal constraints, your company (and you,
personally) can wind up in court.

It is beyond the scope of this book to discuss legal issues, but I urge you to familiarize
yourself with the basic laws related to termination. If your company does not offer this information routinely to managers, suggest that it
does so.

In general, the following are legally allowable reasons for firing an employee. (Remember, you should always consult with your
human resources people before you take action, no matter how obvious the situation
seems to you. In most cases, you will need doc-

umentation of the person's misconduct or performance failure. "I just don't think he was doing a good job" doesn't stand up to a legal challenge.)

1. Unsatisfactory attendance/punctuality
2. Incompetence or inefficiency
3. Negligence
4. Disobedience and insolence (i.e., challenging supervision)
5. Unfitness (i.e., lack of qualifications)
6. Dishonesty
7. Violation of company rules
8. Changed requirements of position
9. Misconduct (e.g., intoxication or drug use, sexual harassment, or immoral conduct)
10. Gross misconduct (e.g., fighting, willful destruction of company property, and stealing)

Vague and subjective reasons sometimes surface that are more difficult to justify—things such as "just cause," "behavior problems," or "lacks potential." Not everyone agrees on just what constitutes a reason for termination. An off-duty employee who was fired by one company for driving a motorcycle through the plant after a drinking binge was reinstated after an arbiter viewed the incident as horseplay rather than a malicious act. It's not a perfect science.

Preparing for the Termination

Here are three common considerations before, during, and after you make the cut:

■ *Warning.* Did you give the employee a warning and enough time to improve his or her performance? Firing an employee should be considered a last resort after every effort has been made to resolve the performance problem. Ordinarily, the first step is a clear verbal warning that states what performance change is necessary. If no improvement is noted within thirty days, you must issue a written warning that expands upon the mandatory requirements, gives suggestions on corrective action, and sets a ninety-day period before a termination decision. Company policies on the length of time between warnings and final action may vary, depending on the complexity of the issues and other considerations. (If you are dealing with a new hire in a ninety-day or six-month probationary period, there should be no hesitation to begin proceedings if the employee is not performing or displays poor attitude problems during that period. It can only get worse.)

■ *Timely Action.* Once you've decided to fire the employee and considered all the legal ramifications, then proceed full speed ahead. Delaying the decision or putting the action off may buy time for the employee, but it doesn't help you at all. Once the written warning is issued, the employee may begin looking elsewhere, slack off on the job, or spend time bad-mouthing the company and getting into mischief. The sooner and cleaner the break, the better. The only reason I can think of for delaying the process would be in special cases where you need time to finalize a plan to replace the person. You may need to have some other ducks in a row so you don't temporarily leave a big hole in the organization.

The employee may even resign. If an employee submits a letter of resignation, accept it immediately and initiate the procedural steps to separate. I had such a situation in which, shortly after a discussion of a worker's poor performance, the indignant worker handed in a letter of resignation. It was gratefully accepted, and the severance wheels began to turn. The next day, the employee said he had changed his mind. My response was that it was too late: He had formally resigned and we had accepted his resignation and moved on. Needless to say, be sure to document all actions related to a termination.

Resignation, of course, is not always best for the employee, since it may affect unemployment insurance. It can, in some cases, also affect company benefits such as a contributory savings investment plan, in which a participant who voluntarily resigns may not receive benefits that are based on the contribution of the employer.

■ *When, Where, and How to Fire.* The "when" used to be on a Friday afternoon (and never during the holiday season). I favor Friday, but earlier in the day. Give the employee the rest of the day off. "Where" is ordinarily in your office and is sometimes done in the presence of a personnel representative or other witness. The personnel department has, of course, been fully informed in advance and all legal issues cleared.

As for "how" to fire, you should get to the point immediately, inform the employee that he or she is being terminated, and explain the reasons for the firing (and review the procedural trail and warnings that have been issued). I may begin by simply saying, "Look, I think we both know that this isn't working," and then proceed with the specifics. You should look to your company legal counsel at every step along the way to make sure that you are not on questionable legal ground.

Be prepared and know what you're going to say. Be sensitive to the trauma that the employee is going through—especially if the individual is an older or longtime employee. Be calm, even though the employee may become angry and hostile.

Incidentally, a company will sometimes replace a worker without prior notice. Occasionally an employee will be startled to see his or her position being advertised in the classifieds. The employer may argue that the person was an "at will" employee who could be

terminated with or without cause at any
time. While not illegal, it's not the
kosher way to go fishing for
replacements.

COMES THE CONFLICT

As noted previously, the mention of a conflict suggests a disagreement, opposition of two parties, or collision about to happen. For the manager, it is a stressful time because she is stuck in the middle. Although you may conscientiously be trying to resolve a tense and loaded situation, you may be caught in the muzzle blast. A conflict involves people, and often unhappy people.

Conflicts come in all sizes: the two workers who can't get along, the problem employee who clashes frequently with the boss, and the know-it-all who refuses to take instruction. Your job as manager is to take control of the situation, act firmly and assertively, guide the resolution (ideally by the parties themselves), maintain calm and flexibility, and seek help when it is needed. Letting conflicts go unchecked can challenge your leadership; furthermore, the effects may be felt throughout the company.

Realize at the outset that in disagreements between feuding employees, as well as between managers, neither side is completely right or wrong. Despite your efforts to seek a fair resolution, there will likely be a winner and a loser. The winner isn't always right and the loser isn't always wrong. Your job is to seek common ground and compromise. Make sure it's an issue of substance to the company and not just a personal dislike, and come up with a solution that has the best chance of making both parties happy.

Ideally, you will ask the warring parties to act like grown-ups and let them settle it themselves. Ask them to fashion a deal and let you know how it was worked out. Once they know that you're fully aware of the situation and that you expect them to act responsibly, their good judgment is on the line. They may equate failure with anything less than crafting a satisfactory solution.

If, however, the disagreement is between a supervisor and her subordinate, and the supervisor reports to you, then you must become more involved. The difference in rank may prevent the two from achieving a truly unbiased resolution on their own. While you must respect the chain of command and be sensitive to not compromise the integrity of the organization, you must also take great pains to protect the rights of each party.

> Most conflicts involve a perceived lack of respect.

I have found that most of what we call conflicts between personnel are the same as those in a marriage or other life situations: One person (or sometimes both) feels that he is not receiving the respect or appreciation he deserves. Poor communication (or no communication) further gums up the situation and prevents its resolution. I mediated a classic case involving a middle manager and her assistant, a dispute that had been described to me as a long-simmering personality clash. When they made no progress in settling it on their own, I brought the two together in a conference room and asked, "What's the real issue here?" After cutting through several layers of incidentals, we reached the core issue. The manager did not feel that the assistant was treating her with the proper respect that her supervisory position merited; the assistant felt that the manager was overbearing, "talked down," and did not treat her with the dignity that a responsible, hardworking person deserved.

We were able to reach a common ground by discussing their respective roles within the organization and recognizing their personal styles and their interdependence on each other. They came to realize that their dysfunctional relationship affected the department and was unacceptable. I think they also were relieved that their boss understood the issue. The manager had harbored some concern that I would question her management ability when the assistant treated her "just like any other employee." The assistant felt that I would think she was not a competent and trusted worker if the manager showed her so little respect. It all boils down to respect.

Any time you bring two participants together, you should keep the focus on them as much as possible. Make it clear that you're just a facilitator and that they need to concentrate on listening to each other.

In resolving disputes with one person or between two or more people, there are some actions you can take that will make it easier for you and the concerned parties:

■ *Watch your language.* Use fewer "why" questions and more "what" and "how." When you ask a person "why" you place the individual on the defensive. "Why can't you cooperate with Charlie?" sets a threatening tone. "What's the situation?" and "How can we work this out?" get the employee involved in the solution.

I knew a trade show manager—one whose job required him to deal with a number of other departments within the corporation—who had an unfortunate liability. In discussions with those customers for corporate services, he often referred to them as "you people." If not outright antagonistic, it served to set up an "us and them" alignment that was hurtful to negotiation. Use friendly words that draw people in, not turn them away.

Watch out for any barriers that your language may be building. Avoid hard words such as "never" and "always," if "occasionally" or "sometimes" are more appropriate. And keep your tone of voice neutral and in line with what's being discussed.

■ *Invite dialogue with open-ended questions.* Try to avoid closed questions that can be answered with a yes or no. The person you're dealing with is probably uncomfortable talking about a problem situation and would rather be somewhere else. People are not going to volunteer information as a rule and a closed question leaves them uninvolved. Your job is not to accuse, but to accumulate information so you will understand all the shades of meaning surrounding the conflict. Try queries such as, "How do you think your absence affected the team?" or "How could we have avoided this situation?"

■ *Be an excellent listener.* Not just a good listener, but one who is listening intently and carefully to every word. Your body language should reinforce that. Respond from time to time to show that you are tuned in and empathetic with a comment such as, "That must have been frustrating for you," or "You sound like that made you angry." Employees want to know that they are being heard and that their emotions are being understood.

■ *Don't pin the tail on the donkey.* Don't fix blame. Your main concern is asking the employee's help in solving the issue, not in pinning guilt. Remain neutral and open-minded, although you may help illuminate the path to a conclusion by reminding about the consequences in doing things wrong and the benefits in doing them right. Avoid applying pejorative terms such as "lazy," "careless," or "foolish" that can personalize the discussion and have a lasting negative effect. Treat people with respect during the conflict-resolution process, bearing in mind that one of the principal reasons for conflict in the first place was the employee's concern about lack of respect.

■ *Seek common ground.* Find the common ground, and then build on it. Find an objective you both agree upon, and then search for the paths to get you there. Flush out as many options and alternative solutions as you can and then determine which are workable and acceptable. Remain flexible and expect compromise.

■ *Assert your needs and feelings.* Asserting your own personal needs as the manager is not taking sides in a conflict. It is explaining your position without disputing theirs. Without blaming or criticizing the employee (or employees), you are simply stating how their behavior makes you feel. These are sometimes called the "I" statements. Begin by stating a factual occurrence, followed by something such as, "When you two managers don't give each other feedback, I feel frustrated because your employees come to me for answers they should be getting from you. Then I have to stop what I'm doing and rush around to bring them up to date. What can we do to change this situation?" I like to occasionally ask, "What would you do if you were in my chair?" and let them get out of their skins and look at the situation from the boss's point of view.

■ *Ask for help.* Finally, realize that you can't solve every conflict. Don't hesitate to seek help. Your company should have other expert resources available. If the situation requires, the company may offer to mediate or arbitrate issues. The American Arbitration Association can also provide an informal arbitration system that allows the company to detach itself from the dispute. Arbitration is the other end, the far end of the street from where we started, which was empowering employees to work it out for themselves.

CRISIS TIME: WHEN THINGS GO BUMP IN THE NIGHT

Surface at once, the ship is sinking!

—*SUBMARINE COMMANDER*

It's revealing that the Chinese character for "crisis" is actually a combination of two symbols—those meaning "danger" and "opportunity." That's not evident to most businesspeople, who tend to see only the danger. The inherent opportunity was evident, however, to Johnson & Johnson in dealing with the Tylenol scare of years past. Pulling the product off the shelf immediately was critical, and so was the CEO's up-front visibility. But also valuable was the quick establishment of a crisis hotline for people with questions and concerns. This service became so valuable, in fact, that the toll-free system remained in place for other emergencies and has been used during hurricanes as a public service for emergency information. It underscores again the need for continuous company crisis planning and its speedy implementation.

Why Should You Care?

Why should you as a manager be concerned about eventualities over which you have no control? One reason might be that company officers and key personnel are increasingly personally liable for any consequences resulting from failure to have taken appropriate preventive or corrective steps. Although the probability is low, the public profile becomes very high when true crises do occur, and—as they say—"it only takes one."

In the case of my employer, Beckman Instruments, there was more than one. Those events included bomb threats, a kidnapping, a large earthquake, hurricanes, several major environmental incidents, and product liability cases. Before you conclude that "Chicken Little was right," let me point out that these events, fortunately, didn't happen all at once. Although it sounds like a lot of misfortune, these potentially serious crises are not all that unusual for a large company. It is clear in business today that planning for potentially damaging events is one hallmark of management excellence and that proactive, prepared companies will minimize the risk of loss— whether it's loss of property, personnel, or the company's reputation and market position.

Defining a Crisis

A crisis has been described by the legal eagles as "an unexpected event that has the potential for a material adverse effect on the company or its employees." To bring that into focus, such an event could result in:

- Fatalities or serious injury
- Environmental damage
- A major evacuation
- Terrorism incidents
- Substantial property damage
- Product failure or recall
- Serious business interruption
- Loss of public confidence

The kind of events that could trigger these dire consequences include a fire, flood, or explosion; earthquake; hurricane, or tornado; an environmental accident, spill, or uncontrolled release of hazardous materials; a product liability lawsuit; kidnapping; bomb threat; civil disturbance; data theft, hacking, and espionage; and other white-collar criminal activity.

Some of these events are assaults from outside or "acts of God" in which your company just happens to be the innocent victim. Ordinarily, the public will be sympathetic and view such an unfortunate event in that context. Others, though, are self-inflicted or may have been exacerbated by negligence or slow response on the company's part. The classic question rears its head in those situations: "What did you know and when did you know it?" Regardless of the root cause, external or internal, your company needs to have a crisis team designated and a crisis plan prepared. Don't wait until you have a problem on your hands to take these steps. When you're mired in the middle of a full-blown crisis, such as Ford Motor Co. and Bridgestone/Firestone have been with the tire recall, with several thousand telephone operators on duty in the Ford crisis management center, there's little else that can be done except furious damage control.

PLAN . . . PREPARE . . . RESPOND!

Your crisis plan should include conscientious planning, preparation, and response plans for handling the emergency. If any leg of the triad is weak, the company is at risk. Henry Kissinger once said, "Next week there can't be any crisis. My schedule is already full." It would be nice if we could schedule these things, but they will occur at absolutely the most inopportune times. The best we can do is be ready with a realistic plan for handling whatever befalls.

Planning: Playing the "What If" Game

To be prepared for a crisis, you can begin by playing the "what if" game. List all possible crisis situations and scenarios and ask yourself, "What if this happened? What would I do?

What immediate decisions would I have to make? Who would I have to call?" (And don't skip over the nuances, such as "What if this event happened on a weekend when the plant is closed?") Computer technology can greatly assist in simulating what if scenarios.

> Ask yourself, "What would I do if this happened?"

Preparing for these possibilities is not an exercise in clairvoyance. It's pretty simple logic. Take the easiest example, and one for which you've probably already prepared: fire. It gets a lot of attention, and rightly so, since fire is the most costly safety problem in the U.S. populace, with losses in life or injuries exceeded only by traffic accidents. A bare-bones fire emergency plan for each company site will include:

1. *A prioritized list of phone calls to be made in the event of fire.* The list should identify who should make the calls and begin, of course, with the numbers for the fire department and other emergency personnel.
2. *A company fire emergency organization.* Year-round assignments should be in effect for:
   - Inspection of fire protection systems
   - Command of initial firefighting and rescue until the fire department arrives
   - Evacuation plans and instructions
   - Utilities shutoff instructions
   - Salvage and cleanup of volatile materials
   - Restoration of fire protection systems
3. *A plan for regular safety inspections.* The plan will call for weekly inspections conducted of the facility and equipment.

4. *Assurance that all sprinkler valves are locked open and that closures are red-tagged.* If any valves are closed, contact the appropriate fire emergency person.

5. *Risk protection.* All protection plans will be reviewed by the insurance company.

6. *Evacuation plan.* Ensure that personnel have the plan and understand it.

7. *Verification.* Be certain that fire drills are held at least annually.

This simple example covers only the planning considerations and steps to take in preparing for the eventuality of a major fire. To deal with the actual fire, your operating plan must also contain a sequence of actions to be taken, by whom and when. This sample outline, with modification, may apply equally well to the handling of explosions or hazardous materials leaks. Other areas for plan development can include procedures for dealing with concerns as dissimilar as boycotts and bomb threats, alerting authorities on issues of employee health, or dealing with adverse publicity.

Your first job as a manager in the crisis planning process is, in a nutshell, to make sure that there is a planning process. If your company has no plan for such emergencies, you bear an obligation to press for one. If a planning process is in place, your role is to contribute to it in all areas of your expertise and to satisfy yourself that it adequately covers your assigned area of managerial responsibility.

Preparation: Going Through the Warm-Up

Preparation is a natural progression from the crisis planning stage and merely arms the plan and puts it into the ready mode. Your managerial role is to take charge of your sector and ensure that every requirement of the plan is addressed and that the people who will implement the plan are fully prepared to do so. Many people will be ho-hum about a fire drill or any other kind of drill, but these emergency exercises are absolutely vital. Even with wonderful evacuation instructions, clear maps and diagrams, and an alarm system that could wake the dead, experience shows that the organization that conducts periodic emergency drills is the one that gets the job done quickly and safely.

Response: The Rubber Meets the Road

If planning and preparation have been properly addressed, the actual response and implementation of the plan follow on cue. Typically, the success of the result is directly proportional to the quality of the crisis plan, the depth of preparation, and the importance that you personally place on what you are doing. The last point may be the most important. If you tend to be cavalier about the urgency of the situation, success is in jeopardy. Planning and preparation can be well done but will be worthless if you delay putting the wheels into motion. Speed kills, but so does inaction.

CONCLUSION: MANAGING TROUBLED PEOPLE AND TROUBLED TIMES

Change . . . challenges . . . conflicts . . . crises. Of all the responsibilities you shoulder, facing this array of difficulties is a truly unique experience for any manager. You can have all the advanced degrees on your wall and ample informational resources at your fingertips, but surviving catastrophe is something quite different. Facts do not equal wisdom. And wisdom is called for in trying times—wisdom and fortitude. Besides, now that you're attitudinally prepped to seize this moment as just another vital aspect of your job, you begin to realize how lucky you are that dark clouds came along at all.

Remember the maxim that applies to life's trials and confrontations: "What doesn't defeat me, strengthens me." Each successful solution acts as a reinforcement and makes you better prepared for the next. Facing trouble provides an unusual opportunity to certify your beliefs with action. It gives you a chance to apply common sense to uncommon conflicts. It shows others how you respond to pressure.

Bottom line, it marks another plateau that you have reached: Your pursuit of management excellence has led you beyond administrative tasks and organizational skills through the valley of plans crafting and consensus building, and all the way to leadership under fire. Not only do your employees see your leadership in a new light, but so do you. Along the way, you may even discover an optimism like the spirited response of Marine General Chesty Puller, who, when informed that his embattled unit was completely cut off by the encircling enemy, announced: "We're surrounded . . . that simplifies our problem! Now we can attack in any direction!"

When you think you've got trouble, remind yourself that perhaps you've only been handed a wonderfully new and broader range of opportunities. Some managers never get the chance to prove their mettle. Consider yourself fortunate.

INDEX